AIRCRAFT 2000

MILITARY PRESS
New York

AIRCRAFT 2000

The Future of Aerospace Technology

Bill Sweetman

This 1984 edition is published by
The Military Press
Distributed by Crown Publishers, Inc.
h g f e d c b a

© Copyright Campbell Rawkins 1984

First published in 1984 by
The Hamlyn Publishing Group Limited
London · New York · Sydney · Toronto
Astronaut House, Feltham, Middlesex,
England

All rights reserved. No part of this publication may be reproduced, stored in a retrieval system, or transmitted, in any form or by any means, electronic, mechanical, photocopying, recording or otherwise, without the permission of the Hamlyn Publishing Group Limited and the copyright holder.

Library of Congress number 84-60703

This book was designed and produced by
Campbell Rawkins,
The Old Power Station, 36-37 Hamilton Road,
Twickenham, Middlesex, England

Designer: Sue Rawkins
Design Assistant: Alan Price

Diagrams by Hayward Design Group
Picture Research by The Research House

Filmset by Colset Private Ltd, Singapore
Reproduction by
Chelmer Litho Reproductions, Essex, England
Printed in Spain
by Graficromo s.a., Cordoba, Spain

ISBN 0 517 436434

Prologue:

0.1

0.2

0.3

0.4

0.5

0.6

0.7

CONTENTS

THE HISTORY OF THE FUTURE

Flying and fantasy have always travelled together - and when powered flight became a reality at the outset of the twentieth century it did not stop there. Aircraft designers have traditionally begun their dreams with back-of-the-envelope sketches, then gone on to commission much more lavish 'artists's impressions' to deflate the sceptics and encourage the enthusiasts. It does not always work of course and a dip into any major aviation archive will produce lavishly crafted illustrations of aviation dead-ends that never flew.

Meanwhile very few ideas in aerospace are really new and the past contains many lessons for the future. If the prediction made in 1900 (far right) of a personal aircraft of the year 2000 was wide of the mark, today's most advanced personal and business aircraft are proving technologies just beginning to appear on larger aircraft. Northrop's flying wing bomber, the YB-49 (below) actually flew as a prototype before being killed off by bureaucracy but today, over thirty years later, flying wings with aeroelastic airframes are a part of the US stealth technology programme.

Boeing proposed this outsize flying boat (right), three decades before the 747 first flew while many proposals such as this one (bottom) were made in the US during the 1960s for a supersonic transport to compete with Concorde. An American SST never flew but NASA is predicting advanced SSTs and even hypersonic transports travelling at Mach 6 along with 1600-seat wide body airliners.

This book contains many artists impressions created in the 1980s to give at least a glimpse of the shape of aerospace in the year 2000 and beyond. Some are fantasies but the majority are based on hard appraisals of what is happening now, revealing bold new shapes in the sky made possible by the revolutions in the science of materials and computing. There are enough prototypes around today, either flying or in advanced development, to make predicting the shape of aerospace in the year 2000 and in the decades beyond, a less fantastic proposition than that which confronted the visionaries of the past.

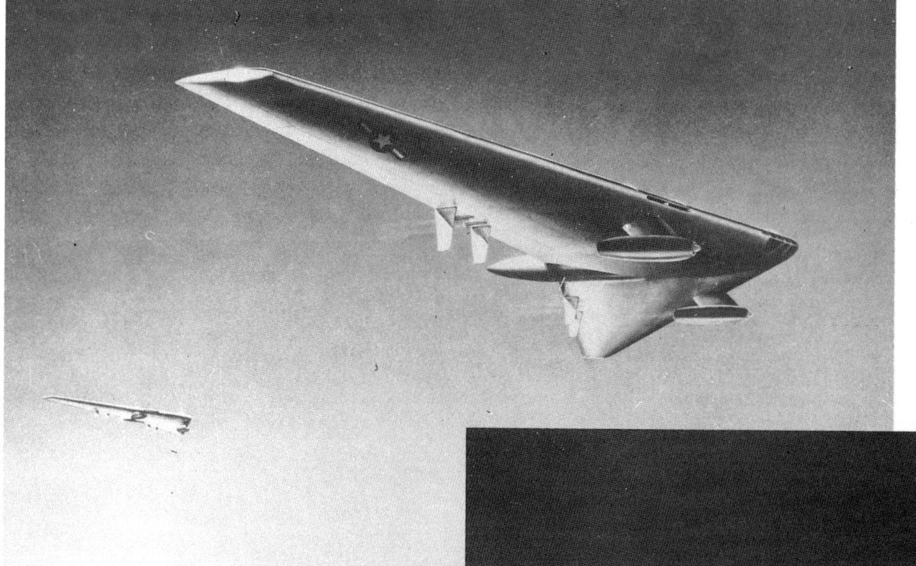

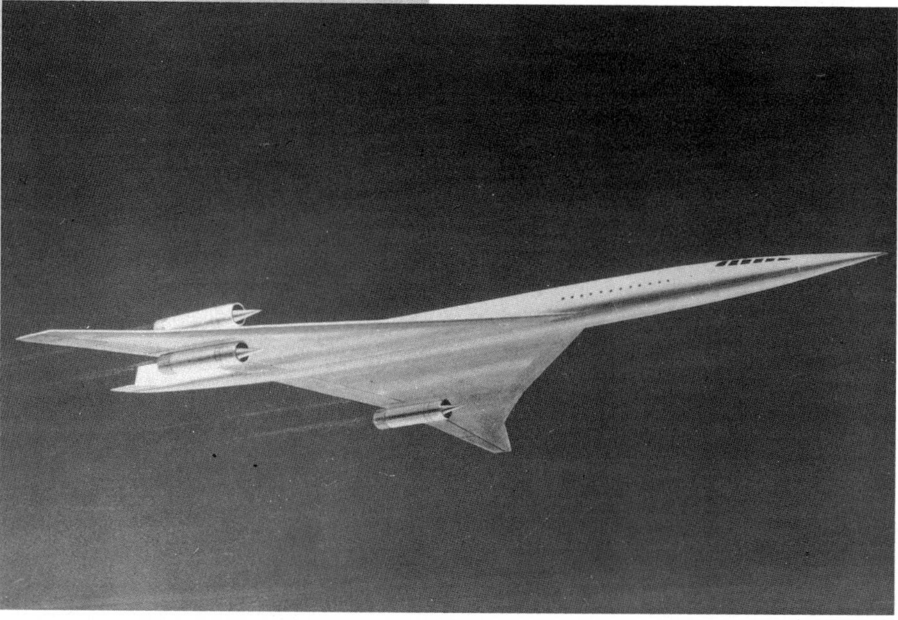

Wings.

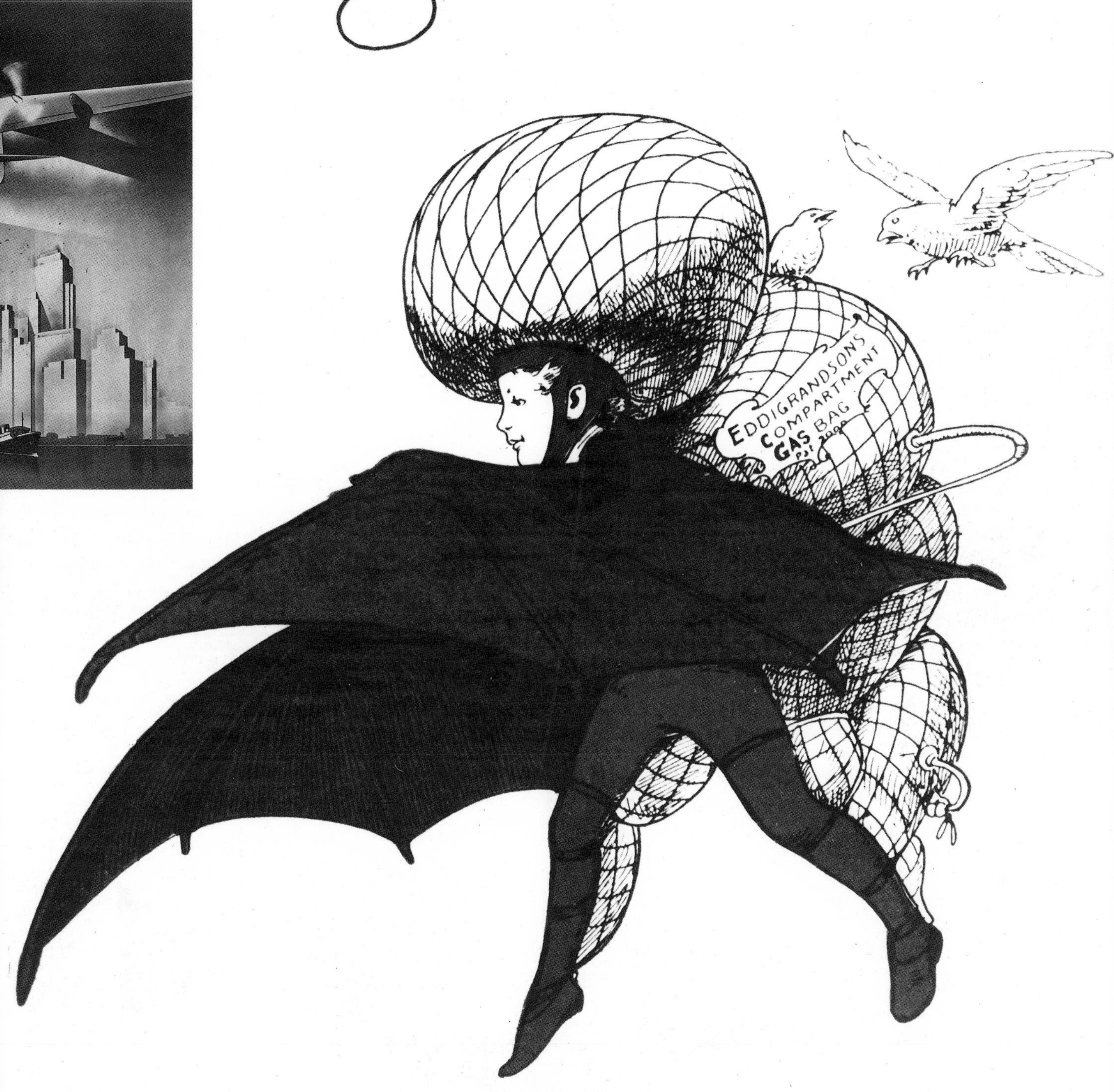

In the year 2000.

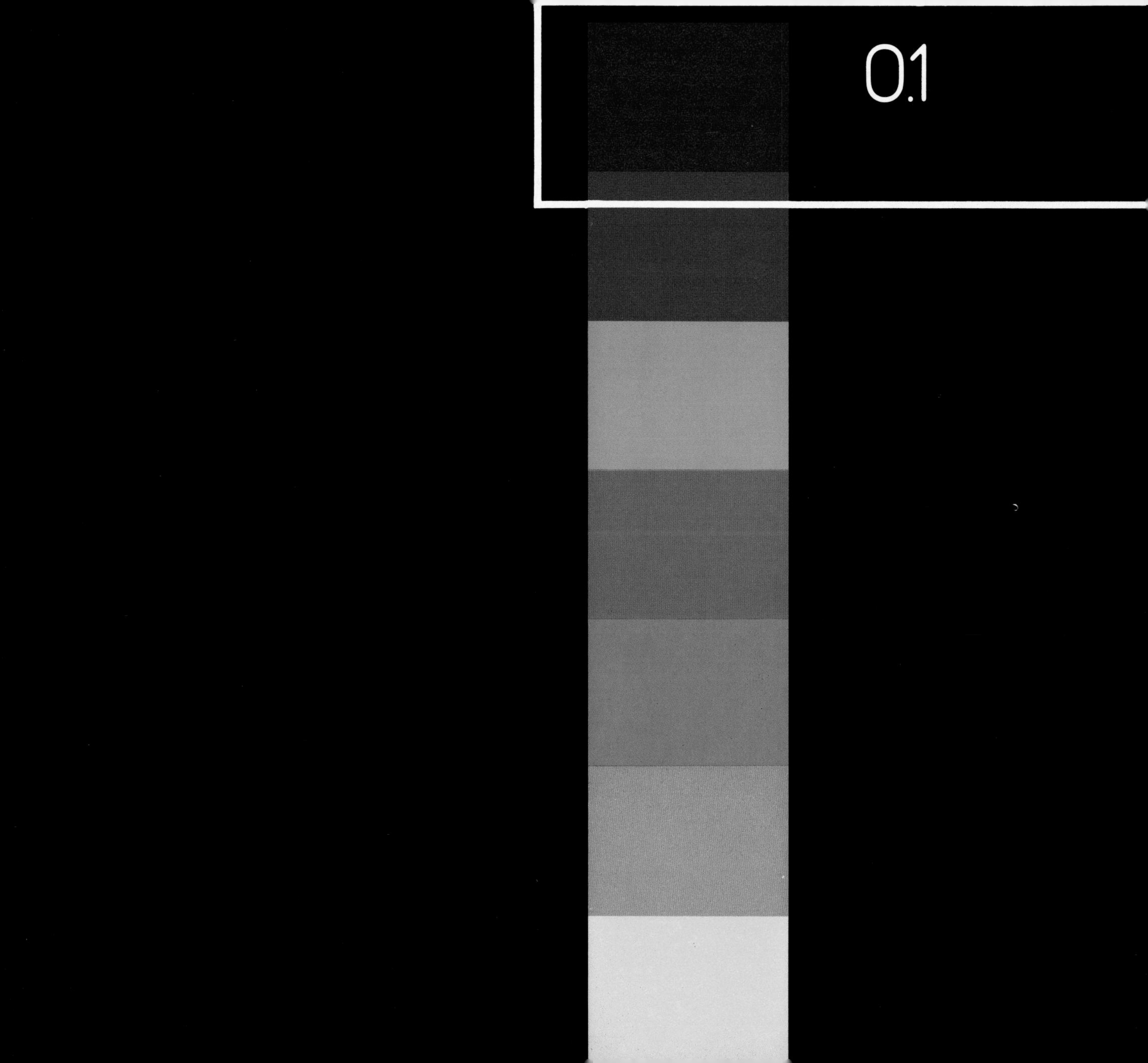
0.1

Building Blocks

Computer controlled machine tool in action

Aerospace is a paradoxical business. From some aspects it seems innovative, generating many new ideas in engineering, pioneering new processes and reaching out for new performance targets. It can also be one of the most conservative disciplines, slow to be convinced of the merits of something new and reluctant to abandon the established way of doing things, whatever faults the established way might have. This paradox has been the secret of the industry's success, and will still be apparent up to the year 2000.

The paradox affects all the broad technologies which contribute to the design of aircraft and space vehicles: materials, aerodynamics, propulsion and systems. Aerospace is innovative, because new technology has always been the way to make warplanes more effective, or to provide more comfortable, more efficient passenger transportation. It is conservative, at the same time, because the consequences of haste, or of taking inadequate precautions in the design process, have all too often been disastrous.

Take the most obvious aspect of the aeroplane, for example: its configuration, or the disposition of its payload, cabin, flying surfaces and engines relative to the wing. The overwhelming majority of aircraft built since the demise of the biplane follow a few standard patterns. The years between now and 2000 will see an increasing number of departures from these norms, and, quite possibly, the establishment of some new standard shapes.

The revival of the canard, or tail-first configuration, is now well under way, and is probably the biggest single configurational change since the monoplane. In theory, the canard is inherently superior to the conventional aircraft, which has a tailplane that pushes downwards in normal flight, effectively adding to the weight of the aircraft. The canard's foreplane, by contrast, is always contributing to the lift. In practice, there have been difficulties with the canard that are only now being overcome.

One problem is to determine the correct 'volume' of the foreplane. In aerodynamic terms, volume is the area of the foreplane multiplied by its distance from the centre of gravity. A foreplane which is too big or too far forward will make the aircraft unstable above a certain speed: if the nose starts to rise, it will just keep rising out of control. But a smaller foreplane will not have much power at low speeds, so if the wing is set at the back of the aeroplane it will not be possible to fit large flaps to it as the nose-down pitch caused when the flaps extend is too strong for the foreplane to cope. Without extensive flaps, the wing must be larger in a canard layout, offsetting some of its advantages.

A few solutions to these problems are now in sight. One is to fit a tailplane as well as a foreplane, the so-called 'three-surface' configuration used on the new Gates-Piaggio GP-180 business transport. The small foreplane is used entirely for trim, not control. It has flaps which trim out the pitch change with flap extension. The tailplane and elevators are used entirely for control. The three-surface layout has also been proposed by McDonnell Douglas for a short-runway version of the F-15 Eagle, and for some of its studies in the Advanced Tactical Fighter (ATF) programme.

Another solution is the variable-sweep foreplane on the Beech Starship I. In effect, this is a variable-volume foreplane, which is swept back to reduce its effectiveness in the cruise. The Starship I, based on an original design by Burt Rutan, also addresses another canard problem, the fact that the wings are too far aft of the centre of gravity to hold all the fuel. Rutan provides the aircraft with big leading-edge root extensions, which put the fuel tankage closer to the centre of the aircraft.

Typifying a point of controversy in advanced subsonic

Left: Extensive use of composites and a pusher propeller combine new technology and old ideas in the highly fuel efficient Lear Fan 2100

Right: The Beech Starship is another contender for the executive transport market of the year 2000. Pusher turboprops are combined with canard variable sweep foreplanes and winglets or 'tipsails'

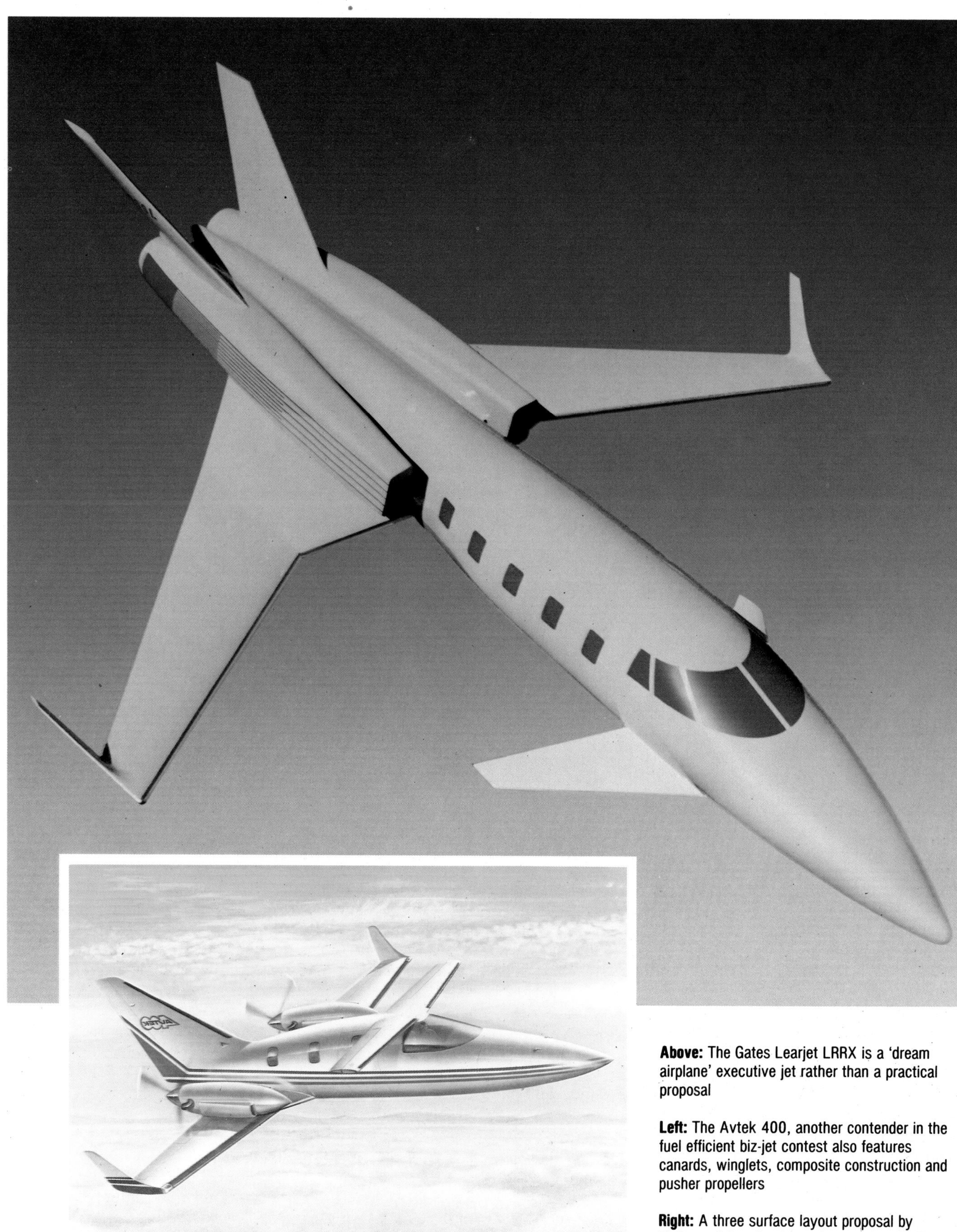

Above: The Gates Learjet LRRX is a 'dream airplane' executive jet rather than a practical proposal

Left: The Avtek 400, another contender in the fuel efficient biz-jet contest also features canards, winglets, composite construction and pusher propellers

Right: A three surface layout proposal by McDonnell Douglas for a short runway F-15

designs, the Starship has winglets or 'tipsails' at the tips of its wings. Winglets remain a point of controversy among designers of subsonic aircraft. Beech and McDonnell Douglas use them on types as diverse as the Starship and the C-17 military freighter; Boeing and Airbus continue to promote efficient conventional wings. Meanwhile, Airbus Industrie's use of a fuel tank in the tail to provide zero-drag trimming, on the A310-300, provides a close approach to canard efficiency for a conventional aircraft.

The Gates and Piaggio designs, and the Lear Fan 2100, also display a feature which will become increasingly common on propeller-driven aircraft: pusher propellers. It has been known for years that pushers are more efficient than tractors, because the high-speed propeller slipstream does not have to battle its way past the airframe. They are also ideal for turboprop engines, which deliver all their power from their rear ends. But until the advent of workable canard configurations it was difficult to 'package' pusher propellers without other design penalties (a big tail, for instance). Future all-new propeller aircraft may well have pushers. The military solution to canard problems, and increasingly to many other problems, is to beat them into submission with electronics. The use of electronics to make an aerodynamically unstable aircraft flyable has two decades of service experience behind it, and its application to canard combat aircraft such as the Israel Aircraft Industries Lavi and Saab JAS 39 Gripen is no longer high-risk technology. Combat aircraft configurations are edging into the realm of gross instability. Grumman's X-29A fighter technology demonstrator is a case in point, with a highly unstable layout and powerful control surfaces.

INSTABILITY SWEEPS FORWARD

The X-29A is also the first aircraft in two decades to feature a forward-swept wing (FSW). With present technology, an FSW is claimed to be significantly more efficient than a sweptback

wing; the effect is similar to gaining extra wing sweep for a constant weight. While the original aim of the FSW was to provide a fighter with improved ability to sustain a tight turn at speed, current advanced-fighter requirements have moved away from this aspect of performance. However, the FSW may well see other applications if the X-29 programme is a convincing success.

Another aircraft which foreshadows the shapes of the year 2000 is General Dynamics' F-16XL, with its 'cranked-arrow' wing. Originally designed for a supersonic airliner, the F-16XL wing provides a unique and attractive combination of low supersonic drag, because the sharply swept inner wing falls behind the primary shock from the nose, and excellent handling at all speeds, due to the powerful control surfaces on the outer wings. The chances are that future military 'supercruisers' (and future supersonic transports, should that concept re-emerge) will have very similar wing planforms to the F-16XL. One feature of the F-16XL design is that it makes extensive use of vortices, spilled from the fuselage/wing junction and the leading-edge kink, to increase lift at high angles of attack. In fact, the designers of the XL assert that vortex lift and the other features of the aircraft eliminate the need for a canard, and hence the weight and drag of the extra surface.

A very important influence on the shape of combat designs today is Stealth, or reduced observables. Blended shapes, used successively on the Lockheed A-12/SR-71, Rockwell B-1 and F-16, will become the norm in military aircraft, because they are efficient as well as helpful in reducing radar cross-sections. Generally, military aircraft will become cleaner, with right-angles faired over and all outcrops and protuberances carefully suppressed. Some aircraft in which Stealth is the top priority will take blending all the way, and become either flying wings or lifting bodies.

Variable geometry, of one kind or another, will continue to be used for some specialised applications. Whether many new variable-sweep military aircraft will be in service in the year 2000 is questionable, simply because existing aircraft will still fill many of the requirements to which the technique is suited. A promising and potentially important technology, though, is smoothly variable camber. This has been an unattainable goal of aerospace for decades, and is finally being made possible for high-performance aircraft through the development of strong but flexible composite materials. Under the Mission Adaptive Wing (MAW) programme, a General Dynamics F-111 is being fitted with a thin-section wing, fitted with smoothly faired leading-edge flaps and a continuously curved variable-camber trailing edge. Flight tests should have started by the time these words appear.

The MAW control surfaces provide roll control and increased lift at low speeds, like the conventional flaps and slats which they replace. The crucial difference is that they do not cause a massive drag rise when they are deflected. On the F-111 test-bed, they will be operated automatically in several modes. They can be deflected downwards to optimise the wing for higher lift in transonic manoeuvre; they can be programmed to seek the most efficient cruise setting at constant power and altitude; the outboard surfaces can deflect upwards in a hard manoeuvre, to reduce the peak load on the wing (this means that the wing can be more lightly built for the same flight load requirements), and the flaps can also move in response to gusts. In fact, the MAW does many of the things that a variable-sweep wing can do, with considerably fewer complications; it has been featured in a number of advanced fighter studies and may well be featured on the Stealth bomber.

Left: One sixth scale model of the forward swept wing Grumman X-29A undergoes wind tunnel tests at NASA's Langley Research Center. Composites make the stresses encountered by forward sweep bearable

SKEWED WINGS

Oddest of all polymorphic aircraft is the Ames-Dryden AD-1, a NASA prototype with a 'skewed' wing: a one-piece wing that rotates about a central pivot so that one wing sweeps back and one sweeps forward. In theory, the skewed wing provides many variable-sweep benefits with far less weight, because of the single pivot and continuous wing structure, and fewer trim problems. The AD-1 has proved to be flyable without artificial help at low speeds, albeit with somewhat peculiar characteristics. It has been suggested that the skewed wing would be an excellent configuration for a naval air defence fighter, with a high-aspect-ratio wing for efficient patrolling, good low-speed performance and 60-degree sweep for supersonic dash. The skew-wing would also eliminate the need for a normal wing-folding mechanism, but it can be safely predicted that the industry's prejudice in favour of symmetry will die hard.

Another class of new configurations may arise from the need for aircraft which can operate from short or non-existent runways and yet attain higher speeds than a helicopter. Some promising approaches are under study. By 2000, if current plans hold and the US Department of Defense is successful, the Bell-Boeing JVX Tilt-Rotor craft should be well established with all the US services. At that time, the Tilt-Rotor will probably be the only high-speed vertical-lift vehicle with adequate payload and range for a transport mission; it is the only concept in sight at present which seems suited to replace long-range helicopters in commercial operations.

Meanwhile, tests with the curious Quiet, Short-Haul Research Aircraft (QSRA), with its four engines above and in front of the wing, are suggesting that it has obtained excellent short-runway characteristics and low-speed handling without sacrificing efficiency in the cruise or adding complicated new subsystems, the two factors which have hampered previous short-take-off and landing (Stol) aircraft. The QSRA uses 'upper-surface blowing' in which the four turbofan engines exhaust over the upper wing surface and the big, smoothly curved flaps. The high-speed exhaust air, and the outside air which it pulls along with it, boost the lift from the wing, and when the flaps are down the jet exhaust is deflected downwards as well, just as water will flow down the curved side of a wine-glass instead of dripping straight downwards.

The Nasa propulsive-lift team at Ames Research Center in California, which managed initial development of the Tilt-Rotor and has produced the QSRA, plans to follow it with a high-speed research vehicle using the same technique, while similar aircraft are under development in Japan and the Soviet Union. Originally seen as a basis for a short-haul jetliner or a military freighter, the QSRA could also lead to new carrier-based aircraft which could land without using the

The General Dynamics F-16XL features a 'cranked arrow wing' providing a combination of low supersonic drag and excellent handling at all speeds due to the powerful control surfaces on the outer wings

The F-16XL is put through its paces in NASA's wind tunnel. Designed-in use of vortices increases lift at high angles of attack and eliminates the need for canard foreplanes

MISSION ADAPTIVE WING

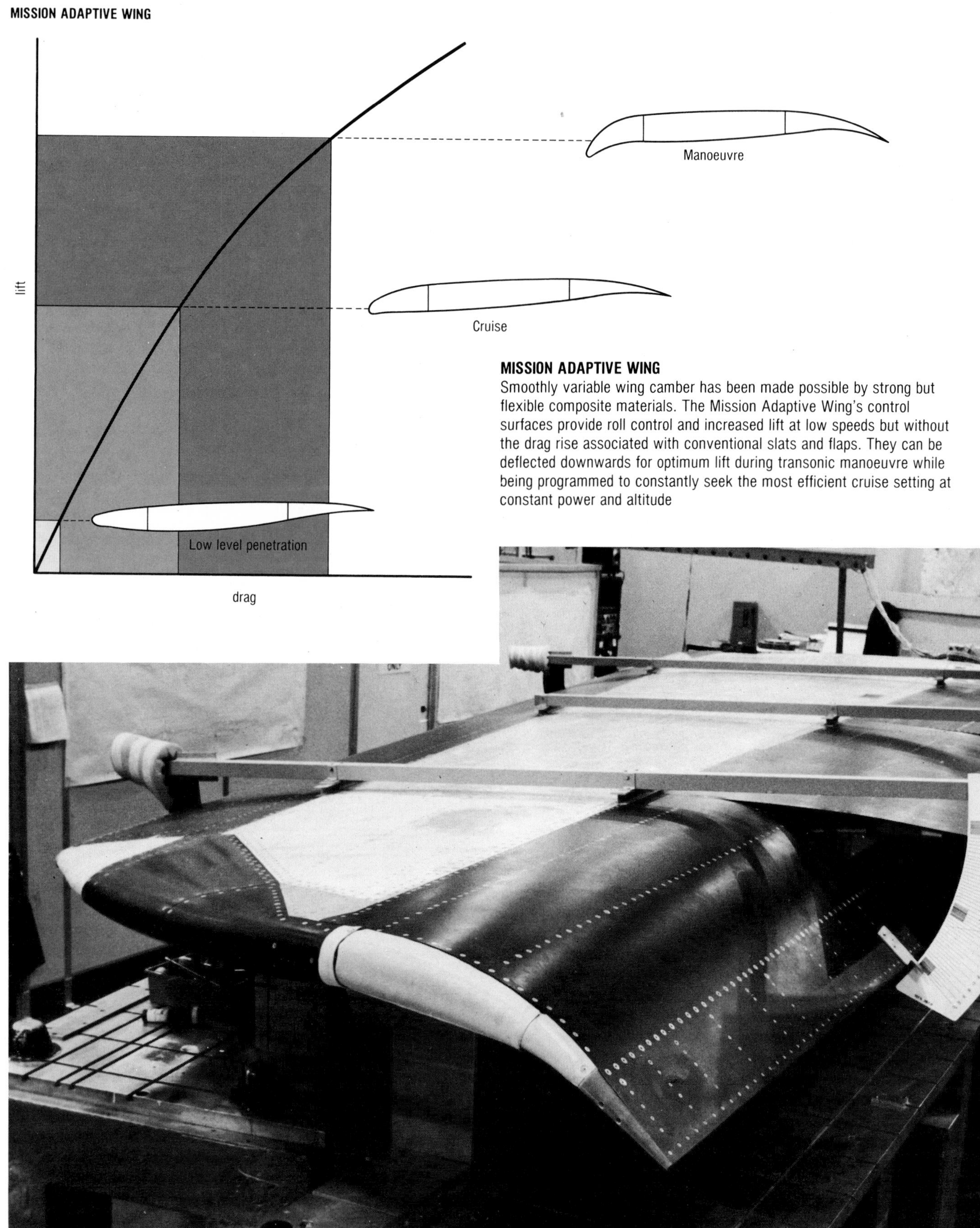

MISSION ADAPTIVE WING
Smoothly variable wing camber has been made possible by strong but flexible composite materials. The Mission Adaptive Wing's control surfaces provide roll control and increased lift at low speeds but without the drag rise associated with conventional slats and flaps. They can be deflected downwards for optimum lift during transonic manoeuvre while being programmed to constantly seek the most efficient cruise setting at constant power and altitude

carrier's limited hydraulic arrester facilities.

An even more outlandish vehicle is the X-wing, a high-speed (450 knots and upwards) machine which might, by the year 2000, be emerging as a successor to current heavy attack helicopters. The X-wing features a completely rigid four-blade rotor which is stopped in high-speed flight, creating an X-planform wing. Making this work properly is even more complicated than it sounds. The air over the rotor blades (or wings) reverses direction as the rotor stops and the aircraft accelerates, so to make them produce lift at all the section has to be changed in flight. This is done by blowing air from specially shaped slots in the leading and trailing edges of the blades. The airflow through the slots will be modulated by valves in the rotor hub, to produce the same effects as control surfaces on an aeroplane or blade pitch changes on a helicopter. In aeroplane flight, for example, the airflow is increased on the port-side wings to roll the aircraft right, or is increased on the front wings to make it pitch upwards. The X-wing needs a special engine, designed so that the energy from its core can be extracted either through a shaft, to turn the rotor, or through a fan for high-speed flight. A full-scale prototype X-wing is expected to fly in the late 1980s, mounted on NASA's Rotor Systems Research Aircraft.

None of these will replace the helicopter, which will continue to be the most common vertical-lift aircraft in military and civil use. By 2000, some new ideas in helicopters may see production. New materials will be used to make simpler, lower-drag rotor systems with more efficient blades possible; on present plans, these are to be featured by the US Army's LHX multi-role light helicopter, to become operational in the early to mid-1990s. Advanced engines and lighter airframes will also make a contribution to lower costs. New helicopter configurations may include the Hughes Notar (no tail rotor), which replaces the drag and complexity of the tail rotor with an aerodynamic device built into the tailboom, and Sikorsky's ABC (Advancing Blade Concept) with its counter-rotating, rigid blades.

At the other end of the speed scale, work continues on shapes for advanced spaceplanes. The current Shuttle was designed with a conservative, and reasonably efficient, double-delta planform, but future vehicles will feature blended lifting-body shapes. (The X-24B, the first successful lifting body, had not been flown when the Shuttle was designed.) Such aircraft will carry heavier loads, and will be able to glide for greater distances after re-entry.

The production of these strange shapes will be facilitated by new materials, many of them being 'composites'. These are in many ways the ideal structural material for an aircraft, and

Left: The Mission Adaptive Wing under development by Boeing. The MAW has no hinged flaps, spoilers or surfaces that break the smooth contour of its upper surface

Above: Ames-Dryden AD-1, the NASA-funded prototype to investigate 'slewed wing' technology. For high speed the wing is pivoted to form oblique 60° angles fore and aft

Above: NASA's QSRA prototype (Quiet Short-Haul Research Aircraft) shows off its excellent low speed handling and short field performance by landing on a US aircraft carrier. The QSRA uses upper surface blowing with four turbofans exhausting over big curved flaps

Left: Technology for tomorrow's helicopters under test on Hughes 'Notar' (No tail rotor) test rig

have decades of experience behind them. They seem to be stronger and more durable than aluminium and should be cheaper to make into aircraft parts. By 2000, aircraft made entirely of composites will be shouldering vital roles in military service, and carrying private pilots and business-people in perfect safety. But it is quite certain that a great many aircraft production lines will still echo to staccato bursts from rivet guns, for reasons which lie in the nature of the industry as well as in the nature of the materials themselves.

COMPOSITE MATERIALS

Composite materials are so called because they are made up of two separate elements: very fine fibres, some of which are only as thick as a single molecule, and a 'matrix' which is poured around the fibres and sets hard. The matrix holds the fibres together; the strength of the material comes from the fibres themselves. The key to the qualities of composites is that very fine, pure fibres can be stronger than a steel strand of the same thickness (everyone remembers the puzzling fact that a spider's web is stronger than steel) and far stronger than aluminium. Even very strong metals such as titanium and beryllium only just approach the ultimate tensile strength of a composite, and are very expensive and difficult to work with; beryllium is light, strong and virtually indifferent to heat, but is, unfortunately, highly toxic.

Glass, or fused silica, was the first material to be widely used in fibre form in composite materials. Some of the latest glass fibres, such as S-glass, show excellent strength and durability characteristics, and glass fibre will continue to have in important place in aerospace. In particular, it has proved so successful in the rotor blades of helicopters that it is hard to see any replacement emerging by the year 2000. Most of the world's helicopter manufacturers, and many military operators, are gradually moving to glass. It is cheap, proven and durable. Its only drawback is that glass is elastic, that is, it stretches under load, and cannot be used for large structures where rigidity is vital, such as the wings and fuselages of large aircraft.

The best known of the new fibres, though, is carbon. Filaments of carbon were first produced in the 1960s, and proved

Left: Joint DARPA/US Navy proposal for an X-wing shipboard helicopter

Right: Lockheed's X-wing test-bed. Locking the rotor in high speed flight provides an X-plan form fixed wing but making it actually work is far more complex than it sounds

Right below: Helicopters will be transformed by composite material technology as much as fixed wing aircraft. This is Sikorky's filament winding machine capable of laying Kevlar Fibre at 36 metres per minute

extremely strong and not unreasonably costly. Carbon-fibre composite (CFC) usually consists of carbon fibres embedded in an epoxy resin matrix, related to some advanced adhesives; in the USA, CFC is known as 'graphite-epoxy' or simply 'graphite'. Its first use was a disaster. Rolls-Royce decided in 1967 to use CFC fan blades on the first RB.211 engine. The blades would be lighter than titanium and, because CFC is stiffer than titanium, they could be made into different, more efficient shapes. While the blades did not fail, the composite material was broken down by the high-speed impact of raindrops on the moving blades. No cure for the problem could be found, and the entire CFC-blade project had to be abandoned. The resulting delay and cost escalation in the RB.211 sent Rolls-Royce into bankruptcy.

Since then, CFC use has steadily expanded. The US Navy's latest fighter, the F-18 Hornet, has CFC wing skins (the wing spars are aluminium and titanium). In 1983, the US Marine Corps took delivery of its first AV-8B Harrier IIs, with a wing made almost entirely of CFC. The newest jetliners, the Boeing 757 and 767 and the Airbus A300-600 and A310 have CFC rudders, and 1984 should see the certification of the Lear Fan 2100, which as far as is known is the first all-CFC aeroplane. In the following year Beech expects the certification of its Starship I, which will use a large percentage of CFC in its production. Tactical fighters are likely to be the next all-CFC production aircraft. The British Agile Combat Aircraft prototype, to fly in 1986, will be primarily made of CFC, as will any production derivative of the aircraft.

A 15 to 20 per cent improvement in structure weight as the material is stronger, so a smaller weight of it will carry the same load, is only one advantage of CFC. Some of its characteristics are more like those of steel than aluminium; it is, for example, somewhat stiffer than aluminium, so CFC structures tend to be less susceptible to flutter. It is also very tough, surviving impacts which would badly damage an aluminium structure. For instance, one of the Lear Fan prototypes was struck by a flying spanner when an over-inflated tyre exploded in its hangar. The spanner bounced off the fuselage into the hangar roof, with so much force that it took two people to remove it. The aircraft was undamaged.

CFC is usually produced as a fabric, impregnated with resin, and like any fabric it has highly directional strength characteristics. A 'basic' CFC structure is made up of several laminations, laid up so that the long fibres run at different angles. But this aspect of CFC is exploited in a design process called 'aeroelastic tailoring' to make structures behave in a completely new way. The best example of this technique in action is the Grumman X-29A fighter technology demonstrator. The skins of the X-29A's swept-forward wing are laid up so that most of the long fibres are aligned slightly forward of the leading-edge sweep angle. A dressmaker would say that they were 'cut on the bias', and like a bias-cut garment they have specific and predictable shearing behaviour under stress. As the wing bends upwards at the tips, the upper skin, under compression, tends to shear forward while the lower skin, in tension, shears aft. But the skins are prevented from moving, because they are both rigidly fastened to the wing spars and ribs, so the shearing forces resist the tendency of the swept wing to twist as it bends. It is aeroelastic tailoring which makes the X-29A and the X-wing practicable, and the technique is likely to be

applied to many other configurations and aircraft types.

COMPOUND CURVES

As composite technology matures, the methods of building in composites will change. The AV-8B wing, for example, is held together by conventional mechanical fasteners (rivets and precision snap-head bolts) like a metal wing. With composites, though, it is possible to lay up separate components, such as skins and stringers, as a single unit, and cure them under heat and pressure simultaneously. The result is essentially a single component, with no mechanical fasteners needed; this saves weight and money and eliminates many of the holes where structural failures can start.

One effect of composite construction will be to make aircraft shapes cleaner and more curvaceous, because composites can easily be moulded into compound curves which metal will only take with a great deal of work. Due to its toughness and the elimination of fasteners, composite material tends to produce clean-looking aircraft.

While CFC is the 'leading brand' of composite material at present, there are other contenders. A class of artificial fibres, known as aramids or polyimides and typified by the Du Pont company's Kevlar, shows a great deal of promise and is being used on two fairly large experimental aircraft: the Avtek 400 business turboprop and Boeing Vertol's Model 360 helicopter.

Advantages of Kevlar over CFC include the fact that it is easier to use; CFC has to be 'cured' under heat and pressure, in a vast pressure-cooker called an autoclave, and, because the resin is cured by heat, CFC fabric has to be kept in cold storage before use. Kevlar is processed at normal temperatures. Together with Du Pont's Nomex, it also makes an excellent honeycomb material. It is, however, more elastic than CFC, and less suitable for highly loaded components: the Avtek 400, for example, has CFC wing spars.

Other composites are aimed at special applications. Carbon fibres can be laid up in a special matrix which is cured at extremely high temperatures, so that it carbonises. The resulting material is called carbon-carbon, and is currently used for parts of the Space Shuttle Orbiter and the nose-cones of ballistic missiles. Carbon-carbon of higher structural quality is now being developed, and could be used in the nozzle and afterburner sections of advanced jet engines as well as in future spaceplanes. Current work on carbon-carbon is mostly classified as is work on 'metal-matrix' composites. As their name suggests, these materials are made up of nonmetallic fibres, such as carbon, in a matrix of metal rather than epoxy. Metal-matrix composites could provide an extremely strong structural material for advanced aircraft by the end of the century. Still more highly classified are plastics and other materials formulated to absorb radar waves.

At the opposite end of the cost spectrum from such exotic products could be other composites based on glass fibres embedded in thermoplastics. These could be extremely cheap

Composite airframe components can be worked into older generation aircraft. This Jaguar (above left) features a carbon fibre engine door while the AV-8B Harrier II (right) has been redesigned around a carbon fibre wing affording greatly increased payload and performance

to produce on a large scale being injection-moulded, literally, like plastic toys, and would be ideal for missile or drone airframes. A system of this kind, using a foam plastic which forms its own smooth outer skin, is used on the Boeing Pave Tiger drone, and Northrop has proposed a tactical stealth missile to the USAF using moulded airframe technology. A prospect for the 1990s could be the application of such techniques to personal aircraft, resulting in an aeroplane which would be cheap to buy, cheap to maintain and aerodynamically efficient.

Large, lightly stressed aircraft such as airliners and military freighters, though, will probably continue to be primarily made of aluminium alloys, for a number of reasons. Possibly the most important is that such aircraft are designed to last much longer than fighters or business jets, flying for 5000 hours a year for two decades or more. Substituting composites for metal in the primary structure of these aircraft would mean a massive programme to prove that composites have no vices that will emerge after 80 000 hours in the air. There is also an enormous investment in experience and equipment behind the manufacture of large, light-alloy airframes.

Staying with metal is becoming more attractive with the development of new aluminium-lithium alloys, claimed to be ten to fifteen per cent stronger than current blends and to be better in other ways, with greater crack-resistance, improved toughness, and less susceptibility to corrosion.

Possibly the most careful of all aerospace people are the engine designers. Generally, a new engine takes longer to develop than an airframe, and engines also tend to stay in production longer than the aeroplanes they were originally designed to power. The aircraft, or at least the manned aircraft, of 2000 will mostly be powered by recognisable descendants of today's engines. The gas turbine, the basic unit around which all jet, turbofan, turboprop and turboshaft engines are built, is the aerospace industry's greatest achievement, having been developed from scratch into an efficient, reliable energy generator that has challenged marine steam turbines and diesels and ousted them from many applications. The process is not over. Work is now under way on the aero-engines of 1995 to 2000. They will be lighter and more efficient than today's engines and, interestingly, substantially less complicated and more reliable.

The engine business does not move quickly. The most advanced engines in service in 1983 were developed from types that were first committed to production in the late 1960s; examples being the big-fan engines which power wide-body airliners, and Pratt & Whitney's outstanding F100 fighter engine. Before these engines were ordered in quantity, their basic features had been checked out on relatively cheap, non-flyable technology demonstrator engines, which had been test-run in the early and mid-1960s.

SUPERCRITICAL WINGS

At that time, the science of aerodynamics had advanced to the point where the flow around a lifting surface, or aerofoil, could be calculated and predicted in two dimensions, as represented by a drawing of an aerofoil section on a flat sheet of paper. In the late 1960s, though, aerodynamicists began to use computers to predict real, three-dimensional effects. These new techniques formed the basis for the advanced aerofoils, sometimes described as 'supercritical', which are used on current aircraft wings.

Every blade in a turbine engine is an aerofoil, but it has taken longer to apply the same new design techniques to engines. The results are now apparent to some degree in new commercial engines, such as the Pratt & Whitney PW2037 which enters service in 1984, and the bigger PW4000. They will be even more visible in two new military engines, the PW5000 and the General Electric GE37, which are being developed in parallel to power the USAF's Advanced Tactical Fighter. Design features of these engines, and of similar demonstrator units developed by other companies, will be echoed in engines in every category by the late 1990s.

New-technology engines will use advanced aerofoils, incorporating carefully calculated twist along the blade span. Each short, thick, contoured blade, and each stage of the engine, will be able to compress the incoming air to a much greater degree than is possible with current technology components, and the result is that the newer engines will attain higher pressure ratios, increasing both efficiency and power-to-weight ratio, with fewer stages. The cut in the number of stages means that the engine is lighter, shorter and stiffer; the last-named quality is important, because a stiff engine can be designed to tighter tolerances, improving efficiency. Each stage, too, will have fewer blades, so the PW5000 and GE37 will have less than half as many blades as the comparably sized F100 and F110 of today.

Most of the materials used in the new engines will be similar to the alloys of titanium, nickel and steel which are in use today. The 1970s saw a rapid advance in both materials and processing; innovations included powder metallurgy, allowing engine discs to be produced from blends of powdered metal which could not be alloyed by normal methods, and directionally solidified casting, which eliminated many of the weaknesses caused by crystal boundaries in a cast blade. Development work in the next few years, which will be reflected in the production engines of the late 1990s, will be aimed at reducing the costs of these sophisticated processes. One way to do this will be to incorporate more automation to improve quality control.

One of the main reasons why today's materials technology will be adequate for tomorrow's engines is that improved technology in the basic design actually reduces some of the stresses on materials. If less energy is wasted through leakage between the stages of the engine, for example, the turbine needs to do less work and can be run at a lower temperature. The new blade sections tend to be thicker, reducing tensile stresses and making it easier to design efficient cooling systems. All these features will help make engines more reliable and more durable.

New materials may, however, be used outside the main working parts of the engine. An example is carbon-carbon, which is likely to see some use in the engine's secondary structure, in its augmentor liners and combustion chambers for instance.

By the late 1990s, some new engines for specialised applications may be making use of radically new materials. The most promising class under investigation are ceramics such as silicon nitride, which not only have enough mechanical strength for use in turbine rotors but are also almost impervious to the effects of heat. This means that ceramic turbine blades can be designed with little or no air cooling, greatly simplifying their manufacture. Bench-tests of ceramic components for small engines are now under way, to investigate the actual strength and durability to be expected from the new materials. It is possible that ceramics will make their first appearance in small, limited-life high-performance powerplants such as cruise-missile engines. Alternatively, ceramics may find their first application in light aircraft powerplants, using technology borrowed from the motor industry.

ADVANCED ENGINE CONTROL

Digital electronic engine control (Deec) will be in widespread service by 2000, and today's hydromechanical systems with their myriad pipes and valves will look as quaint as adding machines do now. The maturity of Deec technology will affect engine design in much the same way as mature fly-by-wire has affected airframe design; engineers will be able to design engines much closer to stall limits, with fewer allowances and margins and correspondingly better efficiency, with full confidence that the Deec can handle the situation. Where the two situations are different is that the Deec is not just an extra item of equipment, it replaces something that is heavier, costs more to build and maintain, and is less reliable.

Deec makes it easier to add new features to an engine, because the electronic system can be more easily adapted to control them. One such feature, likely to be standard on new

General Electric's F110 augmented turbofan will power US combat aircraft of the 1980s and beyond but new materials and digital computer control seem set to make the next generation of military powerplants even lighter and more efficient

engines by the year 2000, is active clearance control (ACC). ACC is the use of controlled thermal expansion or contraction to close up the clearances between spinning compressor blades and the engine case. If the gaps are larger than they need to be, air escapes around the blade tips, flowing towards the lower pressure in front of the blade and wasting energy. With ACC, bleed air is used to cool the case, shrinking it closer to the blade tips. In the Pratt & Whitney Thermatic system, the reverse is done; bleed air is used to heat the compressor rotor.

World oil reserves are unquestionably finite, but a great deal of study over the past decade or so has failed to yield any remotely attractive alternatives to hydrocarbon-fuelled gas turbines for manned aircraft. Different energy sources may, however, be used for some specialised air vehicles. Advanced cruise missiles may use special, exotic fuels to extend their range. Some work has been done on unmanned long-endurance vehicles capable of flying for days or weeks on solar energy alone, storing power in batteries for nocturnal use. But studies of liquid hydrogen as a fuel for normal manned aircraft are currently inactive, and could hardly be brought to the research stage by the year 2000.

As in the case of energy sources, some specialised powerplants will see active development for certain applications. Engines for personal aircraft, for instance, have lagged behind in technology and could be made cheaper, more efficient and more durable. A completely opposite class of engine, the ramjet, is likely to be developed in the same directions of higher performance and lower cost, eventually ousting the pure rocket from some of its traditional uses.

As the end of the century approaches, some of the most important but least considered subsystems on the aircraft could be approaching a major change: the replacement of all pneumatic and hydraulic systems by electrical power. This concept, the 'all-electric aeroplane', may be rendered practicable by the development of superalloy magnetic materials such as samarium-cobalt. Used in electric motors and generators, superalloy permanent magnets can replace electromagnets, with a great increase in efficiency, a reduction in size and complexity and a vast decrease in cooling requirements. In the all-electric aeroplane, the engines would be fitted with powerful variable-speed, constant-frequency generators; constant-speed drives, hydraulic pumps and all air bleeds, which sap the engine's power and efficiency, would be eliminated. In the case of a large airliner, literally tons of high-pressure hydraulic lines, and insulated titanium air ducts, could be eliminated. All controls and moving parts would be actuated by electric motors, providing a natural and direct interface with fly-by-wire control systems. Electric pumps would pressurise the cabin.

New configurations, new materials, new engines and new systems promise some major changes in the shape of the aircraft. A common thread which runs through many of them, interestingly enough, is the reduction of complexity, and the elimination of costly mechanical components which, as all components must, each add their own potential mode of failure to the system. It could be that the innovative aircraft of the late 1990s will be one without rivets or bolts, without hydraulic or pneumatic systems, and with simple, rugged engines. There is one factor that has made this all possible, the new industrial revolution, based on the power of computing.

0.2

Computers
- Aerospace Gets a New Technology

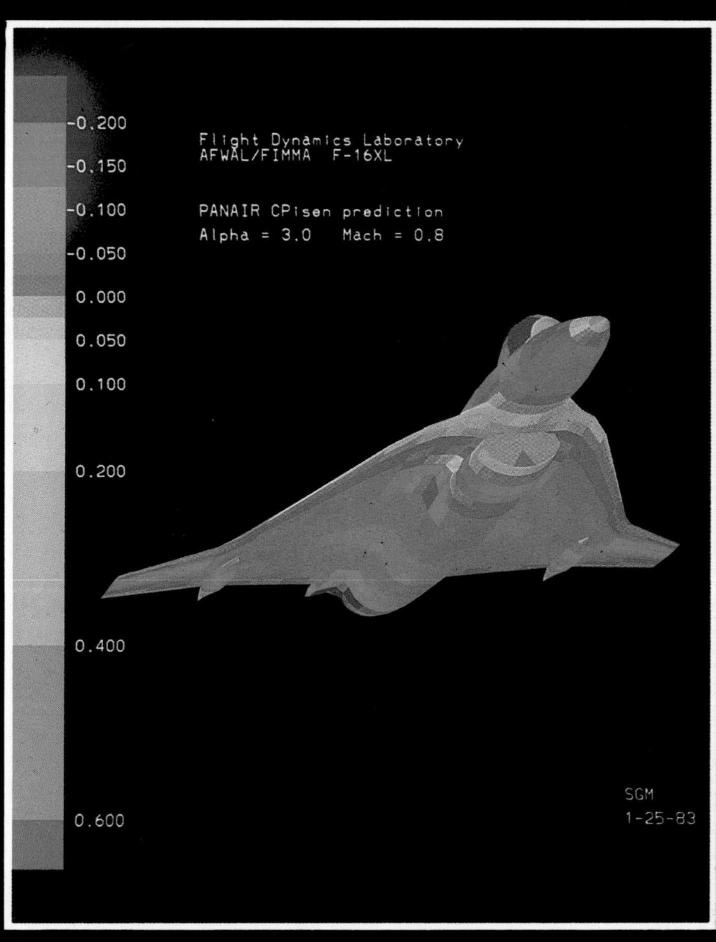

The F-16XL as seen by a digital wind tunnel

ENERGY EFFICIENT BUSINESS AIRCRAFT VIA NEW TECHNOLOGY

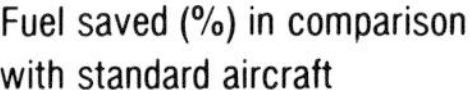

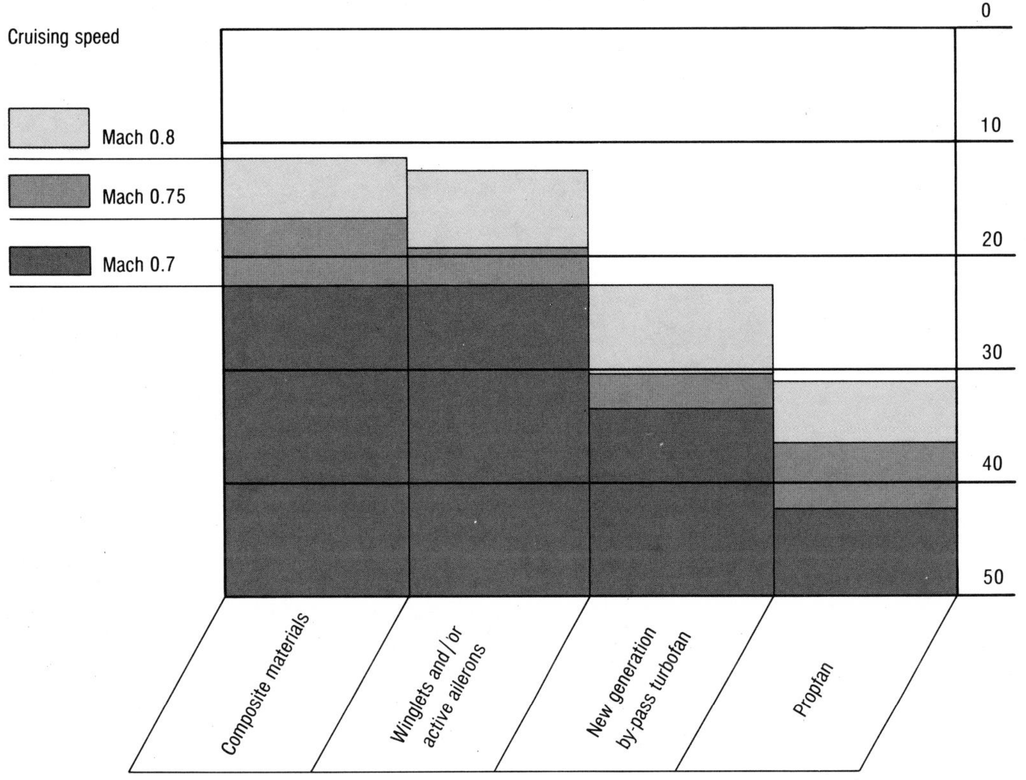

Improvements in energy efficiency which could result from the application of new technology in the business jet field according to a study by Canadair. The figure shows how combinations of technical options produce fuel savings compared with standard aircraft in a speed band from Mach 0·70 to Mach 0·80

When most of the aircraft in production today were being planned and ordered into development, the companies which were doing the planning kept their records on punched cards, 'read' by a complicated electro-mechanical tabulator. The costs of the projects were worked out using mechanical adding machines, each costing as much as a quality piece of furniture. A few of the more fortunate high-grade executive secretaries may even have used electric typewriters which could, to some extent, correct errors. Special air-conditioned rooms of vast size housed a few computers on which time was carefully allotted to each department.

A revolution, for it was no less than that, brought electronic data-processing into almost any organisation, replaced the adding machine by something one-hundredth of the size and dozens of times cheaper, invented word processing and made it affordable, and brought the size and cost of computers crashing down. It all happened in little more than ten years. It is hardly surprising that, to a computer expert, some of the most advanced aircraft now in service, and yet of pre-revolutionary design, seem positively archaic.

Aerospace has always been one of the main forces behind electronic computing. Only a few years after the first computers glowed and hummed into life, advanced aircraft were substituting electronic for mechanical processing, in bomb-aiming devices, for example, and using computers for new tasks such as inertial navigation. Missile and space programmes provided the impetus for electronic miniaturisation. But what happened next was unexpected. Electronic components continued to shrink, and as computer designers used computers to design and build other computers, smaller size was accompanied by higher performance and lower cost. In the 1970s, computing advanced far faster than aerospace could develop and test new uses for it. In the 1980s, aerospace is catching up.

The full incorporation of current processing technology into aircraft will keep the industry busy until the mid-1990s, and will be marked by the operational deployment of aircraft such as the Advanced Tactical Fighter (ATF) and the Stealth bomber. There are a number of reasons why it will take so long.

One is that the application of computing to a multi-faceted, advanced industry such as aerospace leaves almost no part of it unaffected. There is virtually nothing in the industry which cannot be significantly improved by smarter systems of automated control, and it takes both time and money to research and develop advances in so many areas and then implement them as production programmes.

Computing, too, has always been an innovative industry, and shows nothing like the same countervailing conservatism as aerospace. In computer development, the resut of a gross error in programming may be a 'crash', but all that means is that the computer will not operate until a suitably modified duplicate of the original program is written and run. An error of the same type, or even a simple oversight, in the program for a flight control system could destroy an irreplaceable prototype or, at worst, kill a pilot. As aerospace electronics move

out of the realm of gadgetry, and become essential to the safe operation of the aircraft, they must be more thoroughly tested than any previous systems. This too takes time and money.

FLIGHT CRITICAL AVIONICS

The challenge of making such 'flight-critical' avionics airworthy is not just a matter of designing a system that is reliable. One of the biggest tasks in developing an aerospace computer program is defining the degree of reliability needed, and then designing tests which will prove that those standards have been met. The ease of making repairs and modifications, called 'patches', to a computer program has, until now, obviated the need for 'fail-safe' or 'fail-operative' design in software. In the words of a conventional engineer's cynical adage: 'If architects built houses the way programmers write software, one woodpecker could bring about the collapse of civilisation'.

Another important reason for the apparent backwardness of aerospace is that the industry originally based the bulk of its most critical automatic control systems on analogue technology. In an analogue electronic system, changing voltages act as 'analogues' or models of whatever quantity is being controlled or measured: the attitude of the aircraft, the opening or closing of a control valve, or the position of a control surface.

But the computer revolution was based on 'digital' systems, in which quantities were represented by numbers rather than voltages. The development of the microprocessor chip, a purely digital technology, has meant that a digital system can accomplish far more than an analogue system of the same size, permitting new functions to be built in. Its performance can be steadily improved in the light of experience by improving the 'software', or the instructions which set out the relationship between the quantities outside and the numbers which represent them. Digital systems can exchange information more easily than analogue systems, allowing them to work closely together. Microprocessors have proved to be extremely reliable and, moreover, the power of a digital system makes it possible to add a great deal of built-in testing ability. Most digital systems in use or under development today have maintenance modes in which they will find and display any malfunctions, contributing to an enormous reduction in maintenance costs compared with analogue devices.

These and other advantages made the transition to digital technology inevitable, and it is a challenge both to aerospace and computing people. Many digital systems are already in service. New commercial aircraft from Boeing and Airbus have dispensed with many analogue electronic systems in favour of very contemporary and efficient digital technology. In these aircraft, the automatic flight control systems, primary flight instruments and flight management systems are all linked, and draw on a common inertial reference system, which uses digital processing to extract angle and rate information from perturbations in a closed-circuit laser beam.

Where the use of digital technology becomes more challenging, however, is when it is used to perform flight-critical functions which may be entirely impossible with analogue equipment. An example of this technology, now being demonstrated for potential application to aircraft such as the ATF, is the Honeywell digital flight control system (DFCS) on the Grumman X-29A fighter technology demonstrator. Designed for high efficiency at high speed, the X-29A is unstable at low speeds; if it is disturbed from its flight path, its natural tendency is to continue moving away from its original attitude.

Several current aircraft are unstable to some degree, and can be piloted through their full flight envelope only with the aid of their analogue automatic flight control systems. Examples include the F-16 and Mirage 2000, but both these aircraft can fly within certain limits under manual control. The X-29A is far more unstable than any current aircraft, and the DFCS must remain operational at all times.

On the X-29A, it is the DFCS software that defines what movements of the control surfaces take place when the pilot moves the control stick, taking into account the aircraft's attitude, altitude and airspeed. Just to make things more interesting, the X-29A has three sets of surfaces for the pitch axis, instead of the usual one. It has a foreplane, full-span variable-camber flaps, and auxiliary flaps at the tail. The forward-swept wing is itself unique among high-performance aircraft.

The writing and validation of the DFCS software has been the biggest single task in the X-29A programme, more demanding even than the design of the wing. It has involved estimating the response of the aircraft over its entire performance envelope, together with the effectiveness of its control systems, and ensuring that the controls will move to give a constant and predictable control response in the cockpit. The same mathematical model of the aircraft is used in a simulator, together with flight-qualified DFCS hardware, to provide some hands-on experience before the first flight.

Some important questions have to be answered in the process. It is one thing to make an aircraft fly in a stable manner, and another to make it simultaneously stable and responsive. With a control system as powerful as that of the X-29A, too, the designers must judge the points at which the flight envelope should be restricted, balancing the need to maintain flight safety with the requirement to extract the maximum possible performance from the aircraft.

Developing a digital system is a very different task from the development of a traditional analogue AFCS, because of the ease with which the software can be changed. The X-29A, for instance, will be flown with a DFCS program designed to err on the side of safety. Should the designers decide, at a later stage, that more or less response is required in a given flight regime, the necessary 'patch' can be tested on the simulator, and then added to the operational DFCS simply by running a different tape before flight. While the ability to change the characteristics of the flight control system without physical modification is a major advantage of digital technology, it means adding a whole new task, software updating, to the development programme.

HIGH ORDER COMPUTER LANGUAGE

Another aspect of digital systems, which likewise is both a challenge and an opportunity, is the degree to which different components can work together. Most defence authorities are developing high-order computer languages for common use on all military computers, and these provide the basis for levels of integration which are quite unattainable with analogue computing.

The usual means of communication between digital subsystems on board an aircraft is called a 'bus', and gets its name from the fact that it is a single route connecting all the systems. The 'passengers' on the bus are packages of electronic information, each with a special code that identifies its destination. A bus, which physically consists of a single cable, allows any system on the aircraft to talk to any or all of the others, and can thus replace a vast number of individual circuits. As in the case of languages, national and international standards for aerospace buses are being established.

COMPUTERISED AIR COMBAT

A remarkable air combat over New Mexico in August 1982 showed some of the immense potential of integrated systems. The protagonists were an externally unmodified F-15B Eagle and a PQM-102, a remotely piloted modification of a Delta Dagger interceptor. The drone, over three miles ahead of the F-15, initiated the engagement by pulling a 4g turn. Conventionally, the F-15 pilot would have followed the quarry through the turn, trying to close on its tail, but instead he pulled an immediate, shallower turn at higher speed. As the drone pulled through 90 degrees of its turn, the F-15 was approaching in its 'ten o'clock' position, that is to say not quite head-on, at a relative speed between 760 and 810 knots. Both aircraft were still turning as the F-15 pilot fired his 20 mm M-61 cannon at a range of just over a mile, in a 1·7-second, 171-shell burst.

Normally, it would have taken a jet-age von Richthofen to score a single hit against a manoeuvring, high-deflection target, but from what little was left of the PQM-102 it was concluded that it had taken 30 strikes before coming apart. The only modification to the F-15 was the installation of a package of new controls and software called Integrated Flight/Fire Control (IFFC) or Firefly, linking the APG-63 radar and fire control system with the flight control system. The fire control system tracked the target and the predicted trajectory of the shells, and passed 'error signals' to the flight control system. The pilot used the controls for coarse tracking of the target, but the fine pointing of the aircraft was carried out using IFFC. Even more impressive than the live-firing result itself was the fact that the programme managers had not originally expected such effects. At the start of the programme, it was believed that the radar itself would not be accurate enough for automated air-to-air gunnery, and it was planned to fit a TV-type tracker to the F-15. The switch to the radar was made only because the TV hardware proved unreliable.

The Firefly programme has shown what can be done in the air-to-air arena by integrating existing systems with improved software. Another USAF development, based on a modified F-16, is extending the same principle to air-to-ground weapon delivery. Such integration programmes are only a foretaste of what is technically feasible for new-generation military aircraft, and of what is required for such types as ATF. Even a brief description of the avionic system aboard ATF gives some idea of the degree to which computer technology will affect aircraft design.

Above: Getting the sheer mass of target and aircraft management information to the pilot of a modern combat aircraft in a comprehensible way is a problem that only computers can solve. The Thomson CSF TMV980 Head Up Display (HUD) projects graphic information into the pilot's line of sight while the cockpit of this Mirage 2000 accepts voice commands with a 90 word vocabulary

Right: Computerised air combat begins on the ground in highly sophisticated computer-controlled simulators. This F-15 pilot at McDonnell-Douglas's Manned Air Combat Simulator has his wingman, the enemy, the sky and the earth projected onto an enveloping dome screen

Above: British Aerospace's fly-by-wire Jaguar demonstrator

Right: Fibre optic cables are masses of filaments through which information is sent in enormous volume and at the speed of light. They offer high resistance to electro-magnetic pulse (EMP)

Far right: This B-52 is at the top of a huge wooden trestle during experiments on resisting EMP

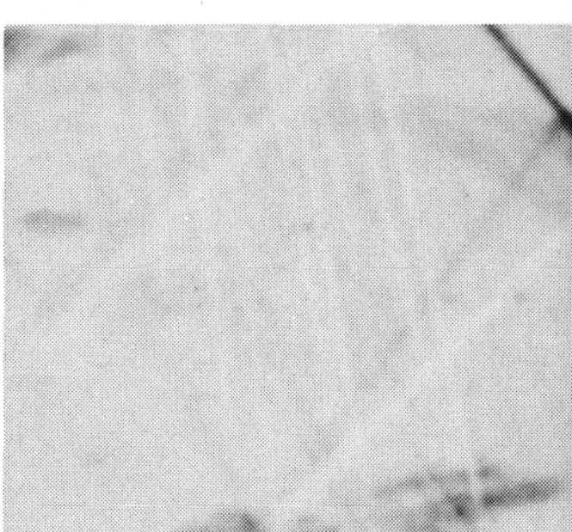

Perhaps surprisingly, ATF will have no central 'master computer' co-ordinating and supporting the entire system. Such a configuration, 'centralised architecture' in avionics terminology, was necessary on some early airborne digital systems, when an aircraft could only accommodate one powerful digital computer. Now that computer power is cheap and compact, it makes more sense to design 'distributed architecture' providing each system with all the processing and memory that it needs. The radar, for instance, can be fitted with a digital 'signal processor' which analyses the raw radar returns and delivers refined data directly to the cockpit display. In-service centralised systems such as the US Navy's A-New anti-submarine warfare system (fitted to the P-3C Orion) are gradually evolving into distributed layouts as new, smarter subsystems are retrofitted into the fleet.

FLY-BY-LIGHT

The links between the various systems will not necessarily be purely electronic. A major consideration in the design of military avionic systems will be electromagnetic pulse (EMP): lightning strikes, or, more significantly, nuclear flash. EMP can cause serious failures in digital systems unless they are insulated and the pulse is channelled around them. Protecting individual control units is not too difficult, but shielding long electrical cables adds weight and complexity, and they are still the weakest point in the system. A strong alternative is optical links, in which signals are converted to light pulses and transmitted along fibre optic cables. These could be used for data buses or to signal flight controls — a 'fly-by-light' system.

The main electronic control systems on board ATF will all be digital. They will include the engine and flight controls, the fire control system and navigation equipment, and systems to generate the symbology projected on the pilot's head-up display system. The aircraft itself may feature a variable-

camber, mission-adaptive wing (MAW), used to reduce drag, increase manoeuvring ability and tighten turns. Its engines will have vectoring and reversing nozzles, primarily to shorten the runway requirement but also used for pitch control and braking. Both will be under automatic control by the digital flight and engine control systems.

In an air-to-air engagement, the fire control and flight control would be coupled for accurate gun firing. The pilot's control inputs would serve to acquire the target and to point the sensors at it, while fine movements would be executed automatically. The flight and engine controls would also be coupled, because thrust vectoring would be used for pitch control and reversing for straight-line deceleration. The entire system would be constantly generating the optimum combination of control surface positions, MAW camber settings, thrust, augmentation and nozzle angle needed to put the cannon shell on the target.

Another intriguing possibility is that digital control systems may be able to adapt to failure or damage, getting the best performance possible from a damaged engine, automatically compensating for asymmetric power or modifying control commands to reflect reduced hydraulic pressure. Such 'adaptive' control systems could allow more missions to be completed, and would certainly ease the piloting task.

Other 'stops' on the ATF data bus will include its electronic warfare system, including both passive (listening and pinpointing) and active (jamming and deceiving) devices. It will be sufficiently powerful to provide useful information to the fire control system, cutting down on tell-tale active radar transmissions. It will draw information from the navigation

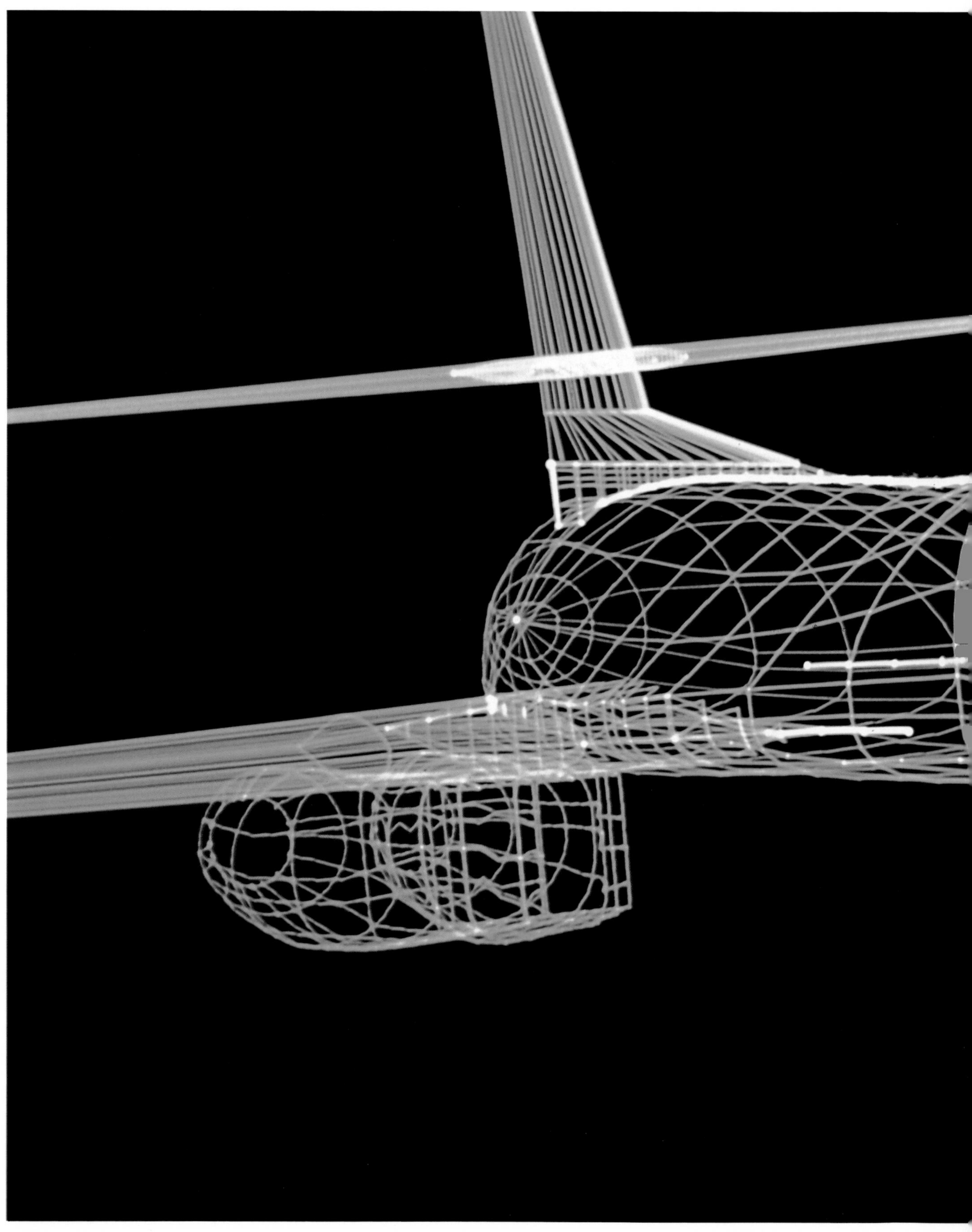

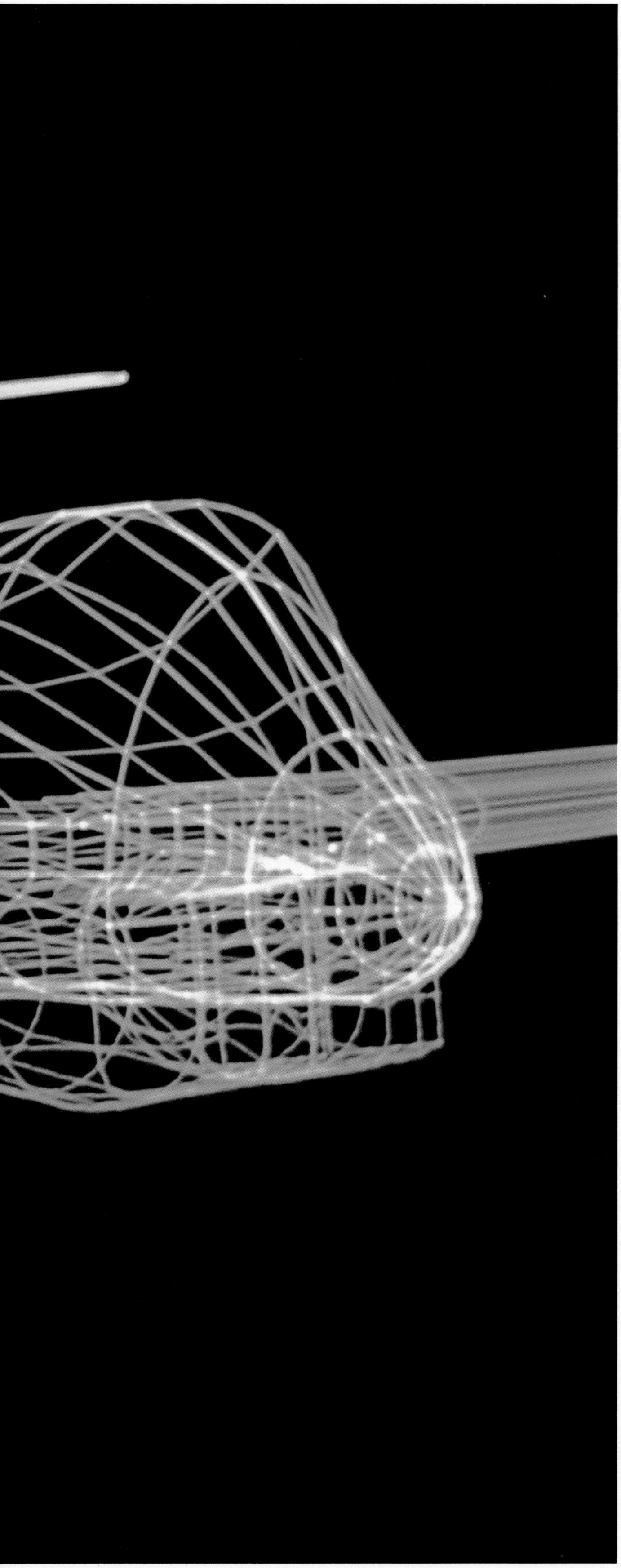

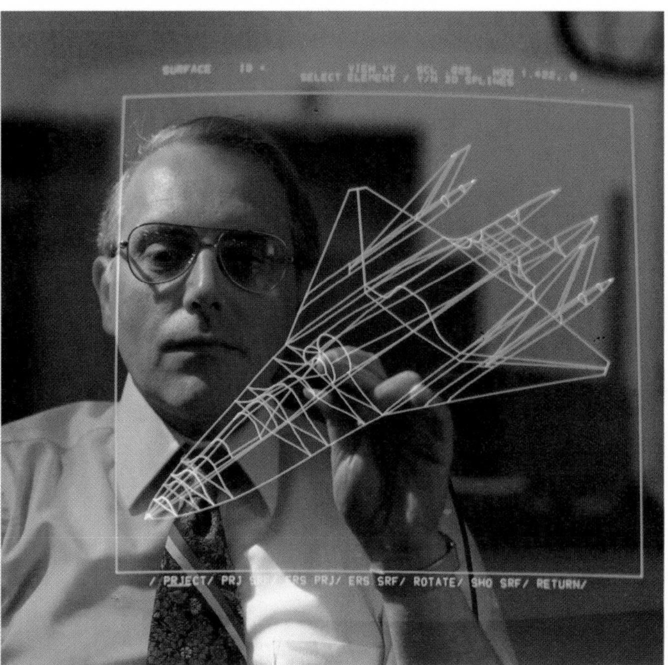

Above: A Grumman engineer works with the computer generated image of an aircraft the blended wingform of which hints strongly at 'stealth' technology

Left: The B-1B, designed in outline in the early 1970s will not enter service until the late 1980s. CADCAM techniques may go some way to shortening ever-longer development lead times

system, for instance, by using groundspeed and course data and taking two bearings on a static radar, it will be able to fix its position and, possibly, pass the information down the bus to a defensive anti-radar missile.

The sheer magnitude of the software task involved is enough to make one wonder whether the development of ATF might not be better managed by IBM than Lockheed or General Dynamics. The notion is not as outrageous as it might sound. IBM is already the 'prime contractor', or leading company, on the US Navy's Sea Hawk and the USAF Nighthawk helicopters, and has competed with airframe companies for leadership of other systems. It is more likely, though, that aircraft companies will develop their own resources in aerospace-oriented computing, with particular emphasis on defining and demonstrating reliability standards, and it is by no means improbable that computer people will fill the programme manager's seat on some aircraft projects by the year 2000.

Most of the examples above have been military aircraft, where the greatest potential and the greatest challenges in avionics are to be found. New commercial aircraft, operating in less demanding environments and with fewer systems, have already made the jump into digital technology, and business aircraft, which in most respects are miniature airliners, are following them.

Commercial aviation will benefit along with the military sector from the increased application of computers to aircraft design and manufacture. One development in this area is

GRUMMAN

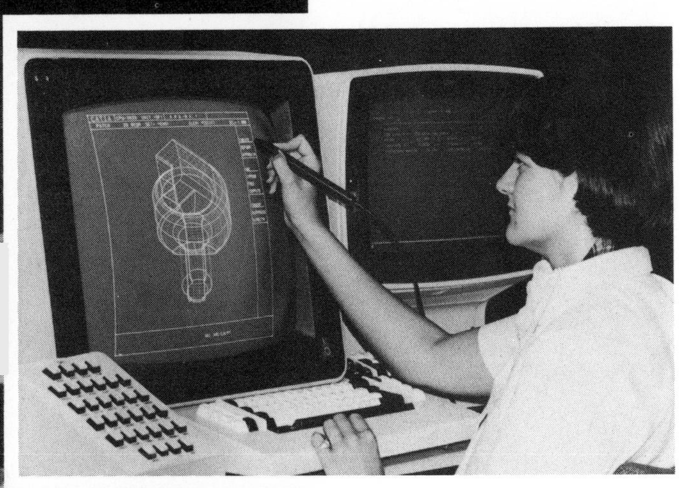

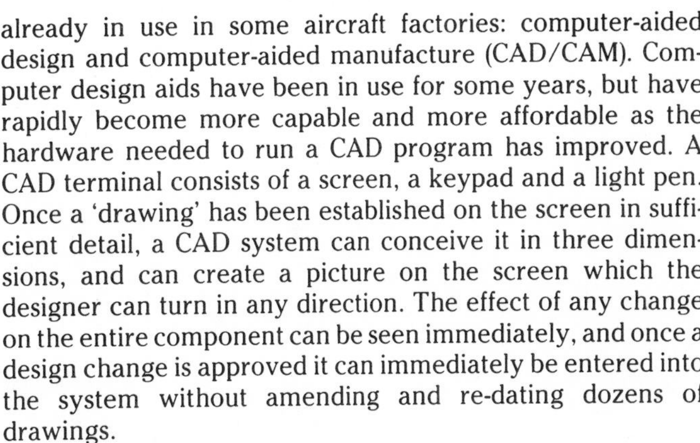

already in use in some aircraft factories: computer-aided design and computer-aided manufacture (CAD/CAM). Computer design aids have been in use for some years, but have rapidly become more capable and more affordable as the hardware needed to run a CAD program has improved. A CAD terminal consists of a screen, a keypad and a light pen. Once a 'drawing' has been established on the screen in sufficient detail, a CAD system can conceive it in three dimensions, and can create a picture on the screen which the designer can turn in any direction. The effect of any change on the entire component can be seen immediately, and once a design change is approved it can immediately be entered into the system without amending and re-dating dozens of drawings.

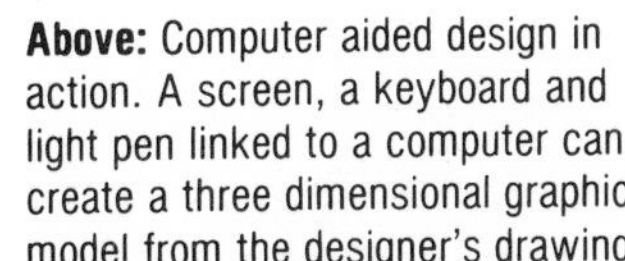

Above: Computer aided design in action. A screen, a keyboard and light pen linked to a computer can create a three dimensional graphic model from the designer's drawing

Left: From computer design to computer manufacture-robotics will increasingly dominate the business of building aircraft. This is Grumman's computerised beam builder

FACTORY OF THE FUTURE

CAD/CAM is the extension of this principle to manufacture, aimed at reducing the currently high cost of aircraft structures. It is being used to cut costs on the US Air Force's new T-46A trainer, by simply allowing machine tools to be controlled by the CAD computer; the information that the designer has put into the CAD computer is used to machine the part itself, eliminating a source of errors and costly delays.

The 'factory of the future' is a step beyond current CAD/CAM systems and about 20 of these units are now operational. A good example is Hughes Aircraft Company's Flexible Fabrication System (FFS) in Los Angeles. The FFS contains ten machine tools and is run by three people. It is used to machine aluminium castings into small, precisely finished housings for components such as missile guidance systems, and Hughes estimates that the same job would take twice as many tools and eight times as many people in a conventional workshop. A central computer not only controls the machine tools, as it would in a current CAD/CAM system, but it also controls the movement of parts from one station to another, using a system of carts running on floor tracks. In this way, the position of each part is known at all times, the flow of work is kept under precise control and the amount of time which each tool actually spends cutting metal is doubled or trebled.

Such completely automated systems will continue to be expensive, but their potential is enormous. For example, the flexibility of computer systems may make it more attractive to use fewer, more complex parts in a system, as it becomes possible to automate their manufacture and still achieve very high quality levels. Another contribution to design efficiency is the possibility of making modifications or changes very quickly, and with none of the 'learning curve' effects common to normal production lines. The automation of parts distribution, transport and control will have a wider application, even to the sort of assembly operation where human dexterity is still required.

In the most basic fields of aerospace technology, computers are on the verge of making yet another major contribution to the industry. At NASA's Ames Research Center, work is under way on a massive computer facility which will be able to predict and map the airflow around a complete aircraft, like a

Above: The mini side-stick controller on the Airbus A300 puts the pilot's hand on the airliner's computerised flight control system

Left: This Thomson-CSF flight simulator for the Airbus 300 is another computer based design tool. Flight commands are interpreted by computer and transformed into real movements via hydraulic rams with the pilot's view entirely composed of computer generated imagery

Right: —and it can be very realistic. This Redifusion SPI Novoview computer-generated imagery allows a pilot 'flying' a Chinook helicopter simulator to perfect the daunting task of landing a big helicopter on an oil rig without leaving the ground

wind tunnel. But the computer, described as a Numerical Aerodynamic Simulator (NAS), will be able to test computer 'models' at full scale, at speeds far higher than Ames' own full-scale wind tunnel. Unlike physical wind-tunnel models which can, including their own engines, cost millions of dollars, these computer models can be easily modified to reflect design changes or alternatives.

The development of systems such as the NAS is being made possible by the emergence of new, faster computers. Up to now, computers have been able to analyse airflow to some degree, but even the most powerful systems available have been too slow to simulate complex flows 'in real time'. Investigating the flow around even a small component, at one instant in time, has taken tens of hours on the best computers available. In computerese, the NAS will need to run at a speed of 'one gigaflop': one billion floating-point operations per second. NASA plans to achieve this in 1988 by linking two current-type, 250-megaflop supercomputers, but gigaflop machines could well appear by 1990. US computer manufacturers are concerned by Japanese efforts to take the lead in this development, and have pressed for government support. Other agencies and companies are working on similar systems, and by the early 1990s they may be the most important design tool in the aerospace industry.

The only clue to the way NAS technology will affect aerospace is the observed impact of the much less sophisticated aerodynamic analysis techniques and systems introduced in the 1960s and 1970s. These led directly to the development of supercritical or aft-loaded aerofoil sections, which have brought about a ten to fifteen per cent improvement in the efficiency of large commercial aircraft, and of the three-dimensional, controlled-diffusion engine aerofoils used in the more rugged, more reliable new-generation engines. One area in which the advent of these 'computer wind tunnels' could be decisive is that of transonic and supersonic aerodynamics. NAS systems are likely to test the 'supersonic persistence' configurations under consideration for ATF, and may even point the way towards transonic and supersonic commercial aircraft with realistic operating costs.

Another computer-based design tool is the flight simulator. Computer-generated imagery (CGI), in which the view from the simulator cockpit is produced entirely by a computer, began to replace the old systems of models and closed-circuit tv (CCTV) in the 1970s, and has now reached the stage where it can do far more than any conceivable CCTV system. Within a few years, in-service CGI equipment will be able to present a realistic outlook for almost any mission; low-level attack in patchy weather against a moving ground target, for example. In an advanced fighter or bomber design, where the only 'central management system' is the pilot, the ability to test the

avionics, displays and the human pilot in advance of the first flight will be tremendously useful.

Airborne and space-based computing, meanwhile, will be moving into another new era by the year 2000, with two new features coming to the fore. The aerospace and defence industries are already moving into the forefront of advanced computer development, by providing the need and the money for the development of faster, more powerful and even smaller computing devices to succeed the microprocessors or 'chips' on which present systems are based. This concept is known as very high-speed integrated circuitry, and is usually abbreviated to VHSIC — pronounced 'vizzic'.

ARTIFICIAL INTELLIGENCE

The other major factor in the future of airborne computing, intimately linked to the development of VHSIC, is the emerging concept of 'artificial intelligence': the development of machines which can think, instead of merely processing data. The distinction is vast. The pilot of a military aircraft, for example, not only takes decisions in fractions of a second, based on his background of knowledge and experience, but can instantly assess if that decision has to be changed a second later (another MiG has appeared) and to what extent. Moreover, at the same time, the pilot is 'scheduling' his actions and even his thinking processes, deciding what must be done now, what must be done next and what can be done simultaneously, and shelving some decisions to a later time. Compare this with the modern systems that are erroneously described as 'smart'. The most that they can do is communicate data, fly a pre-planned or commanded course, or, in the case of a missile, distinguish between 'target' and 'not-target'. Hunting dogs are shot for less.

Experimenters in robotics, the branch of engineering which couples basic artificial intelligence to the ability to take physical action, have created machines which can operate in a much more sophisticated manner, sensing and responding to the unexpected, negotiating obstacles to reach a given goal, and updating their memories according to experience. So far though, such machines work on a 'stop-think-move' cycle, because computer capacity is inadequate to match a constant speed of motion. In the next few years, a team of US Navy researchers hope to have modified an armoured vehicle so that it can follow another across rough ground, a first step towards 'autonomous transit' and continuous motion. But the armoured vehicle's ability to carry a great deal of computer equipment, and its speed, are a far cry from aerospace applications.

With VHSIC, it is hoped, it will be possible to apply intelligent logic to dynamic, constantly changing environments, within reasonable limits of space and cost. In a manned aircraft, artificial intelligence could be applied to the sensor processing and cockpit display systems, co-ordinating the operation of navigation/attack and electronic warfare systems and providing some of the unique capabilities of a two-crew aircraft in a smaller, lighter and cheaper single-pilot aircraft. Using voice-recognition equipment, the pilot could even talk to his robotic back-seater. But it is in unmanned systems that the potential of artificial intelligence is greatest. Genuinely 'smart' weapons (the term 'brilliant' is sometimes used for

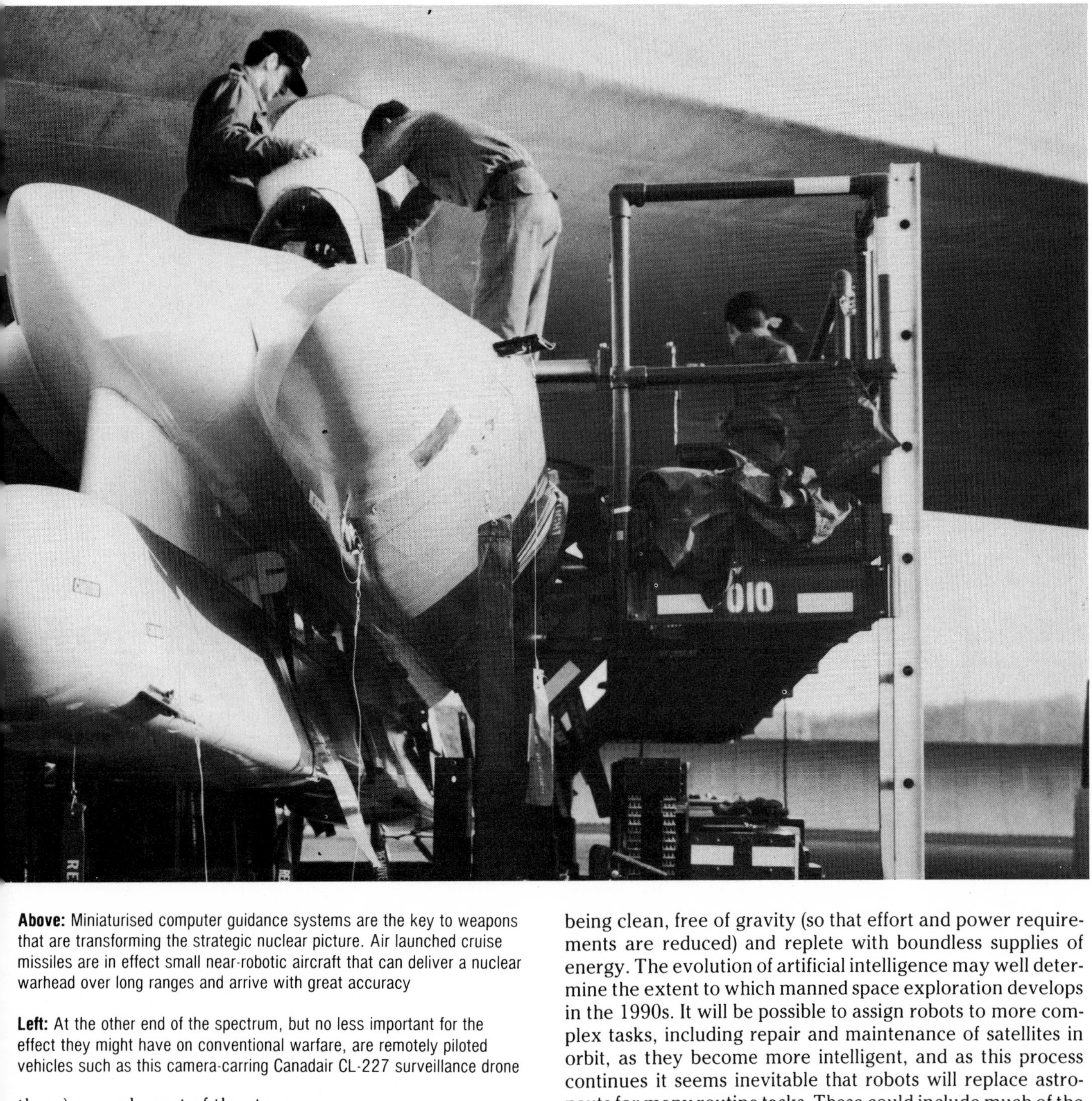

Above: Miniaturised computer guidance systems are the key to weapons that are transforming the strategic nuclear picture. Air launched cruise missiles are in effect small near-robotic aircraft that can deliver a nuclear warhead over long ranges and arrive with great accuracy

Left: At the other end of the spectrum, but no less important for the effect they might have on conventional warfare, are remotely piloted vehicles such as this camera-carring Canadair CL-227 surveillance drone

these) are only part of the story.

Unmanned vehicle systems (UVS) will be used to fill a few of the roles filled by the manned aircraft, but will also create a great many new missions, particularly in hazardous or inhospitable environments, where the risk to the human operator is so great that the cost of the mission is largely determined by the cost of keeping the operator safe. This logic may apply to any number of situations. Military examples might include low-level reconnaissance, attacks on heavily defended airfields or ships, or chaff-bombing in front of an attacking force.

The most inhospitable environment of all for humans is the total vacuum of space, but it is almost a paradise for robots being clean, free of gravity (so that effort and power requirements are reduced) and replete with boundless supplies of energy. The evolution of artificial intelligence may well determine the extent to which manned space exploration develops in the 1990s. It will be possible to assign robots to more complex tasks, including repair and maintenance of satellites in orbit, as they become more intelligent, and as this process continues it seems inevitable that robots will replace astronauts for many routine tasks. These could include much of the work put forward as the justification for ambitious manned space station projects. Greater use of unmanned, robotic vehicles could lead to a new assessment of the need for the costly capability of retrieving orbiting vehicles.

In the year 2000, the status of electronic computing technology in aerospace will be firmly established. From its beginnings as a set of mysterious and unreliable black boxes in a few special-purpose aircraft, it has now become something very different; along with aerodynamics, materials and propulsion, it has taken its place as a fundamental aerospace technology.

0.3

Space 2000

The Shuttle heralds new adventures in space

United States

It is an odd twist of technological history that the future of manned spaceflight may be defined by the development of a technology which originated to support it, but that is exactly what is happening. Micro-electronics, first developed and exploited for the great space adventures in the 1960s, picked up speed on its own in the 1970s and, in the later 1980s and 1990s, will change the shape of space exploration and exploitation.

Robotics, the creation of intelligent machines, is the central development here. While current space systems are largely automated, 'intelligence', or the ability to act on memory and sensed data rather than responding in a predetermined manner to a limited range of stimuli, will be a great step beyond it. It will make spacecraft more reliable, not because their mechanical components fail less often but because the robotic system can adapt to a component failure. It will also greatly increase the number of tasks that can be successfully and efficiently performed by unmanned vehicles.

In the world of spaceflight, robotics is a high-payoff technology. The irradiated vacuum of space is the least hospitable environment conceivable for human beings. Survival means a controlled environment, achieved in a pressure cell or a highly complex and restricting spacesuit. Both must be designed, equipped and constructed to 'man-rated' standards, to prevent so much as a short-time failure, further increasing their cost and complexity. On long missions, human beings require stored oxygen, water and food, and space to move around in, all of which have to be hauled expensively into orbit. Humans must also be brought down from orbit at regular intervals, a process requiring the use of specialised vehicles.

Astronauts will still be critical to spaceflight in the year 2000. Human intelligence will still be needed to operate the Shuttle, and its improved derivatives. The inclusion of human intelligence, with our unparallelled ability to solve unexpected problems, will be both operationally desirable and economically justified in the installation and maintenance of large and costly orbital systems. Experimental and development work will be the astronauts' responsibility as well.

For robots, space is close to an ideal environment. Zero gravity reduces the mechanical loads to be overcome, and what energy is needed is available free, in unlimited amounts. Space is largely free of contamination. Robots can stay in orbit indefinitely, and need no life support systems. The cost of adding redundancy or reliability to an unmanned system can be simply balanced against the likely cost of losses. For many space operations, too, the absence of human contamination is a positive benefit. The economic arguments in favour of using robots in space, wherever possible, are overwhelming.

MILITARY USES OF SPACE

The other major trend over the next decade and a half will be the increased use of space for military purposes and, in particular, the US plan to develop a comprehensive, space-based system of defence against nuclear attack. A word of caution

A permanent manned space station is one of the most enduring of science fiction and science fact proposals while the advent of the Shuttle has moved it nearer reality

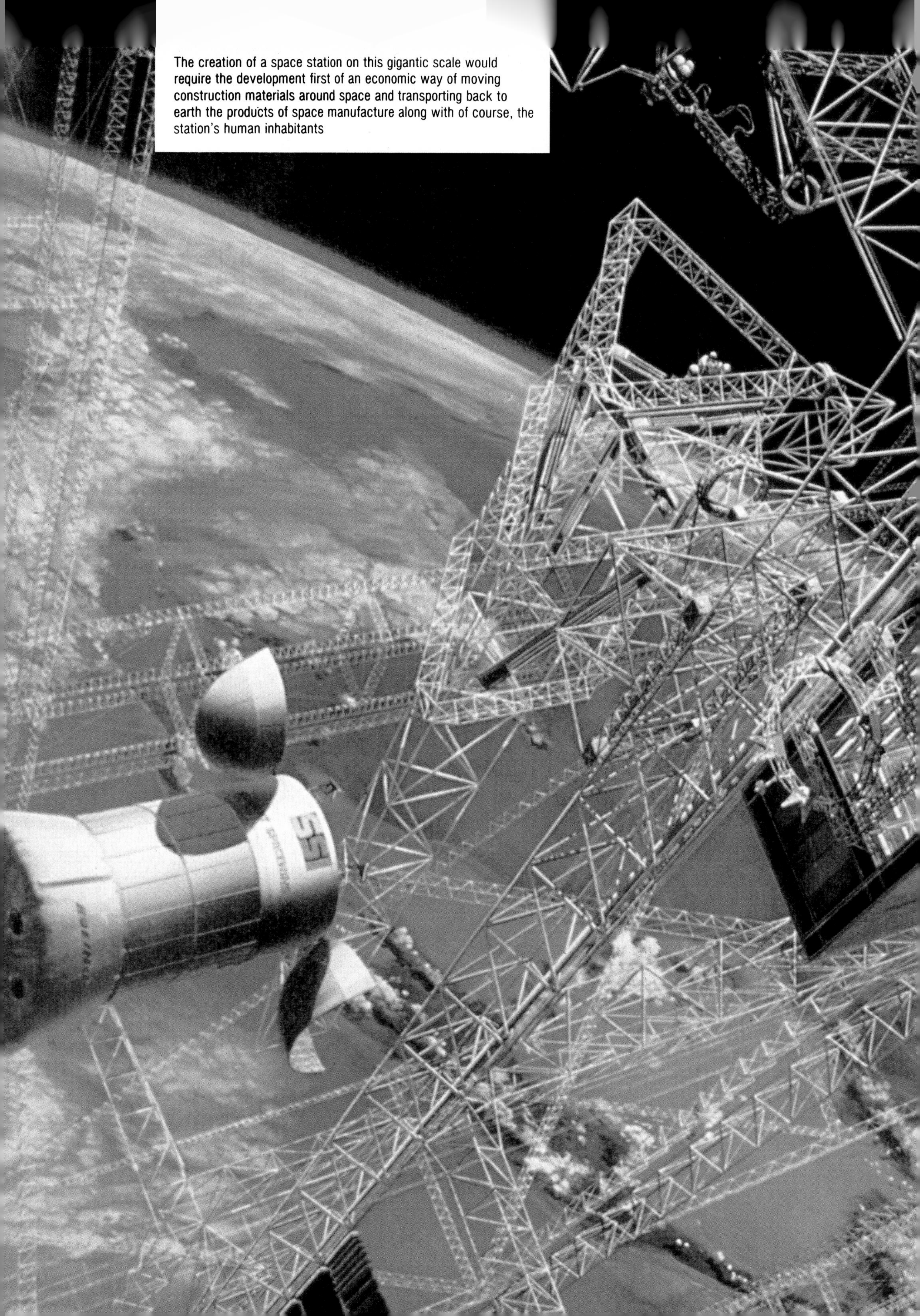

The creation of a space station on this gigantic scale would require the development first of an economic way of moving construction materials around space and transporting back to earth the products of space manufacture along with of course, the station's human inhabitants

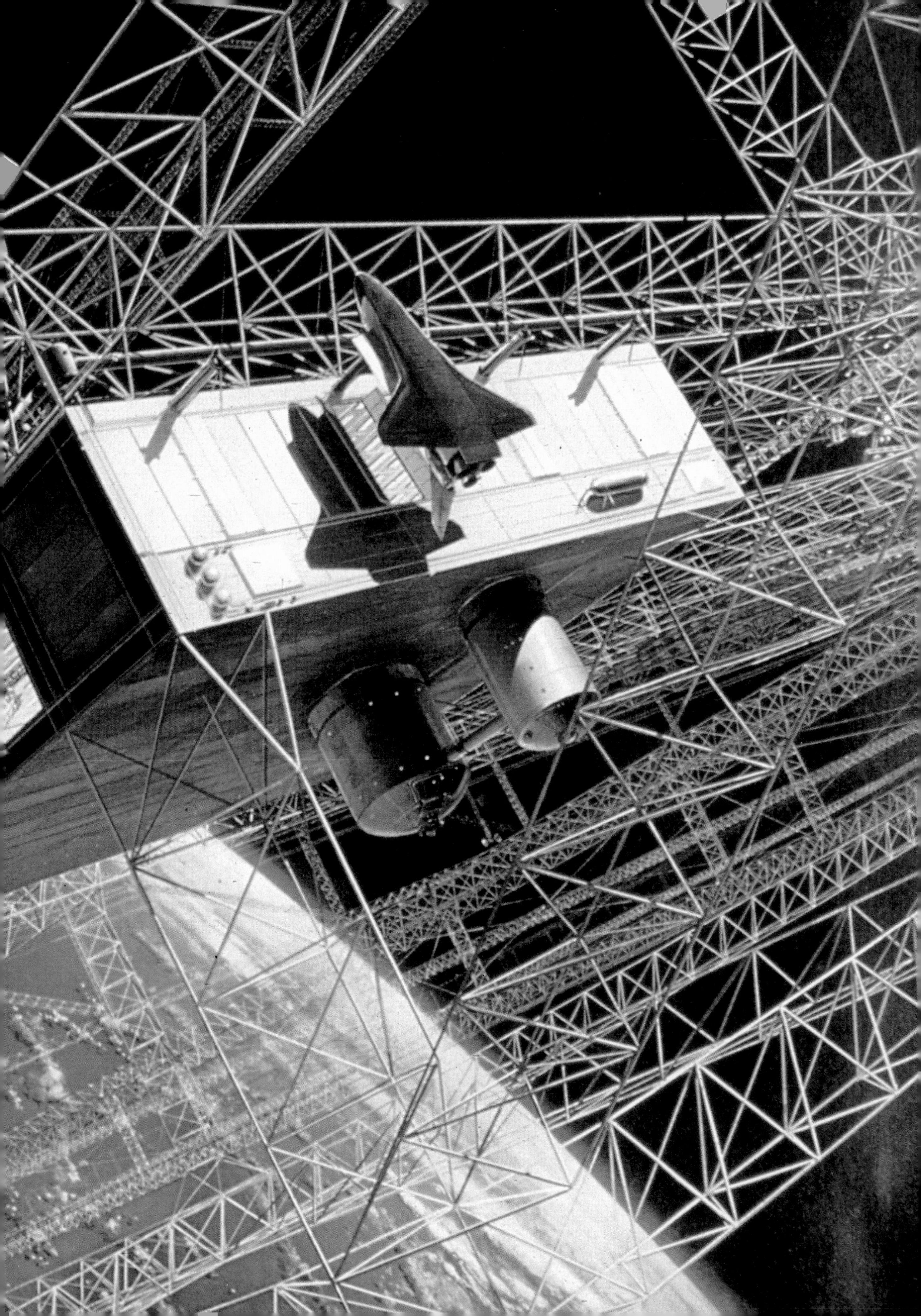

Shuttle mission lift off, a triumphant reaffirmation of the US space programme. The Shuttle has demonstrated its ability to lift 30 tonnes into low earth orbit. An auxiliary cargo carrier under development could double the Shuttle's cargo volume

SOVIET AND US SPACE LAUNCH VEHICLES

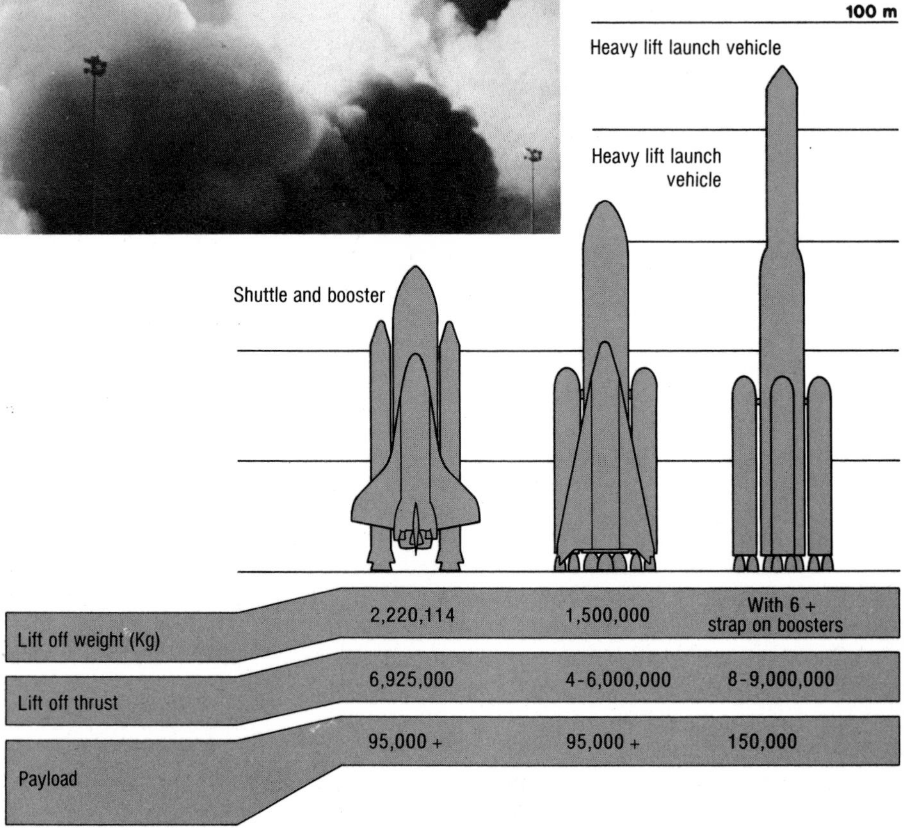

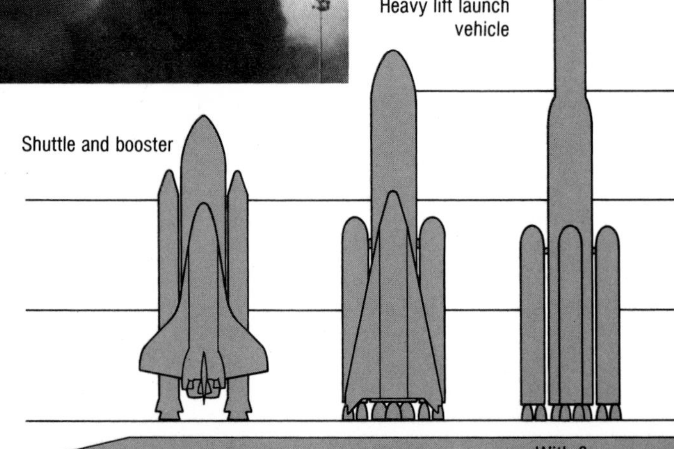

	Shuttle and booster	Heavy lift launch vehicle	Heavy lift launch vehicle
Lift off weight (Kg)	2,220,114	1,500,000	With 6 + strap on boosters
Lift off thrust	6,925,000	4-6,000,000	8-9,000,000
Payload	95,000 +	95,000 +	150,000

Right: How the space heavyweights line up. While the Soviet Union is reported to be following the US path and developing a reusable Shuttle-type space plane, the US Department of Defense has also released its estimate of the giant G-1 booster's capability, able so, Americans say, to put a payload of up to 150 tonnes into a 180 km earth orbit, reflecting Soviet priorities in getting very large unitary payloads into orbit.

should be uttered at this point; space-based defence is a controversial issue, and at least three US presidential elections will take place before its deployment begins. At the time of writing, the last days of 1983, its chances are no better than even. If it proceeds to operational use, however, its financial and technical demands, and its operational and engineering 'spin-off' effects, will dominate space development, just as Project Apollo did in the 1960s.

Robotics will have a very great impact on one of the main technical advances to be expected between now and the year 2000: the development of a space station. This will be very different from earlier experiments in long-term space habitation. Its most important characteristic will be permanency. The space station will have power to prevent its orbit from decay, will be fully integrated with means of resupply, and will be modular in design so that even a severe failure will not affect the integrity of the entire system.

Modular design for the space station means that human habitation is easily added as an option, but that it is not essential to the concept. It will almost certainly be added however, even if partly for political reasons. The space station is likely, though, to be the first application for a space-borne teleoperated manoeuvring system or tug, which may be used not only to retrieve other vehicles but also to assemble modules for the station itself. The modules would not necessarily be linked rigidly to the main structure of the station; they might be connected by cables, or even radio or optical links.

NASA's planning for the space station, at least in late 1983, seemed to be stressing the great variety of uses to which a space station could be put, while avoiding the risks of concentration on any one mission. Until the advent of true artificial intelligence, a module attached to a space station and linked to its information processing equipment and its human occupants by a high-capacity databus, will have a functional advantage over any single-function satellite. At a later stage of development, orbiting systems might be tested under human supervision on the space station before their artificially intelligent control systems were 'graduated' into independent vehicles. The space station could also be a base, either manned or robotic, for the retrieval and repair or rehabilitation of damaged or worn satellites.

Alternatively, there is a good possibility that the space station programme will be diverted and accelerated to serve a specific purpose, such as the strategic defence plan mentioned earlier. The techniques used to establish and maintain the station might be little different, but many of its potential uses would be explored rather later, if at all.

In most cases, large space transportation systems conceived in the 1970s will meet the needs of the 1990s, with limited modifications and the use of some existing components in new configurations. It is now clear that there is room for a number of systems, each best suited for a particular job; the main variables are payload weight and orbital height. There are some basic considerations which govern the prospects for different types of vehicle.

The economic arguments between expendable and re-usable launchers seem to have receded. Originally touted as the replacement for the throw-away booster, the re-usable vehicle suffers a payload penalty due to its aerodynamic structure and its recovery systems. It needs a crew, and its theoretical advantages are further reduced by high post-flight refurbishment costs. Re-usable and expendable vehicles will be regarded as complementary in the coming years, and the main distinction between them will be the former's ability to return a payload and crew from orbit. The Soviet shuttle design, significantly, appears to be a compromise between the two classes. Its main engines are expendable, and attached to its external fuel tank. The orbiter's ability to return payloads from orbit is considerably increased, thanks to the removal of the engines, the substitution of a more aerodynamically efficient tailcone, and the elimination of large payload doors in favour of a smaller tail door.

SPACE SHUTTLE 2000

The current Shuttle has demonstrated its ability to lift 30 tonnes into low earth orbit (LEO), and there is some question as to when and whether the requirement to lift heavier loads will arise, certainly in the commercial and scientific field. As payloads increase in size, they tend to increase in cost, and it may prove more advisable to design systems for orbital assembly rather than risk a total loss. A similar situation applies to payloads destined for geostationary earth orbit (GEO), where today's lift capacities are unlikely to be increased. Instead, modular and orbit-assembled systems will be employed.

Two developments, aside from the planned steady improvement of the Shuttle's engines, may provide a greater LEO payload capacity in the 1990s. One is an auxiliary cargo carrier attached to the rear of the Shuttle's external tank, which would more than double the Shuttle's cargo volume to orbit (but not its recovery volume) at little cost in weight. It could be used to carry awkward, outsized loads. Another development is the Shuttle Derived Launch Vehicle (SDLV), an expendable system using the Shuttle's engines, its solid rocket boosters and external fuel tank.

The Soviet Union is still alleged to be working on its giant G-1 booster, somewhat larger than the Saturn V. Under development since the early 1970s, the G-1 has never been tested successfully, and has been involved in at least one violent mishap. Its continued development would indicate that the Soviet Union sees a future high-priority need to launch an extremely large unitary payload.

New space vehicles may well be developed to improve the ability of re-usable spacecraft to place vehicles into GEO. The only way to do this at present is to use an expendable booster, or orbital transfer vehicle (OTV), to carry the payload up from LEO. Re-usable OTVs, capable of bringing vehicles or components back from GEO, involve a new technical challenge: how to decelerate the vehicle from GEO velocities, in order to rendezvous with the Shuttle for re-entry and landing, without using excessive amounts of fuel. One way of accomplishing this is by outer-atmosphere braking, using inflatable aerodynamic surfaces or a 'ballute', a balloon-type parachute, to decelerate the vehicle on the fringes of the atmosphere.

Towards the late 1990s, though, a completely new class of vehicle could begin to emerge, reflecting and exploiting technical changes and advances in spaceflight and robotics, and changes in the use of space technology. It will be a small, low-payload re-usable vehicle, and would have much greater flexibility and higher performance than the Shuttle. It would be used for reconnaissance, strategic defence and even surface attack. Work on this class of vehicle started only recently, and its definition is by no means complete. In the course of 1983, however, US Air Force planners began to describe it as the 'transatmospheric vehicle' or TAV.

The TAV is a true aerospace vehicle. Its core is a high-efficiency lifting-body, typically carrying a single astronaut and a mission payload, capable of atmospheric re-entry and powered by a built-in rocket or ramjet motor. The TAV could be ground-launched or air-launched with a booster stage and external tanks, or space-launched by the Shuttle. Its operating regime would be limited only by its launch mode and the combinations of boosters and external fuel which would be available, extending from level flight at 240 000 feet to geostationary orbit.

Some of the unique characteristics of the TAV are now attracting very serious interest. In 'endo-atmospheric' flight (within the atmosphere, or below 50 miles altitude) the TAV flies almost as fast and as high as a satellite, but it can manoeuvre aerodynamically, like an aircraft, to evade attack or orient itself towards a target or reconnaissance objective. Satellites can only manoeuvre to the limits of their fuel supply, which is to say hardly at all.

The TAV is a recoverable vehicle, like the Shuttle, but because of its much smaller size it can be far more mobile. In 1982, Boeing released details of an air-launched sortie vehicle (ALSV) under study for the Air Force; while this was not a TAV, it was a related study, and its weight and propellant requirements would be similar. The Boeing ALSV was to be a lifting body with integral motors and an external fuel tank, and was to be launched from the back of a modified 747. The airliner's fuselage would contain the liquid hydrogen and liquid oxygen fuel for the entire mission, in well-insulated tanks, and a Shuttle main engine would be installed in its tail. The 747 would climb to 22 000 feet before filling the ALSV's fuel tank in the cold high-altitude air. The shuttle engine would be fired, and the 747 would climb at a 60-degree angle to 37 000 feet before separating from the ALSV and its tank.

The tactical advantages of a TAV launch system of this type are immense. It is self-contained and mobile, and can be based at any airport with a 10 000-foot runway, a sharp contrast to the vast and vulnerable fixed facilities required by the Shuttle. Due to the insulated tanks, it can sit for days with a full load of fuel on board, and with the aid of air refuelling, the system can launch the TAV from any point on the globe.

The TAV is also more manoeuvrable than conventional space vehicles. A common vehicle would be used for operations within and outside the atmosphere, although it would be fitted with a different external tank system. Launched from the Shuttle, the TAV would be able to fly out to geostationary orbit, perform its mission and return either to its base or to the

Right: This strategic reconnaissance aircraft proposal from McDonnell Douglas uses a transatmospheric vehicle layout to fly at twelve times the speed of sound and at earth orbits more than 1250 miles high

Top right: A high energy laser experiment in progress at a US laboratory funded by the Defense Advanced Research Projects Agency which is working actively on directed energy weapons

Left: Technicians fit a re-entry vehicle to the warhead-carrying post-boost vehicle of a US Peacekeeper (MX) ICBM. The development of multiple warheads in the 1960s effectively truncated anti-ballistic missile development. Now the Reagan administration has called for a great research effort to develop an effective space based anti-missile screen around directed energy concepts as illustrated above

Shuttle. It would be equipped to allow extra-vehicular activity, so that it could be used to perform maintenance or repair on satellites; it could also defend against anti-satellite systems and act as a low-vulnerability substitute satellite.

Development of the TAV will call for advances in aerodynamics and thermal protection. The USAF Flight Dynamics Laboratory has proposed the development of a trans-atmospheric demonstrator, the manoeuvring re-entry research vehicle (MRRV), either manned or unmanned and designed for free-fall launch from the Shuttle or boosted launch from a B-52. It would be a small lifting-body vehicle, only 25 feet long; candidate shapes include a straked conical configuration, originally conceived by nuclear-weapons specialists at the Sandia Corporation as a possible manoeuvring intercontinental ballistic missile (ICBM) re-entry vehicle, and the wedge-shaped FDL-5 designed by the USAF Flight Dynamics Laboratory. The latter uses a Lockheed-developed technique called 'compression sharing' in which pressures across the vehicle are carefully tailored to obtain hypersonic stability without the weight and drag of excessive fin area. Thermal protection could include carbon-carbon primary structures or Shuttle-type tile systems. The TAV would also require innovations in other areas including compact, flexible navigation and flight control systems designed to handle extreme circumstances; and lightweight, long-endurance life-support systems.

While the foregoing discussion has outlined some of the potential of the TAV, military requirements and considerations of cost, time and feasibility will determine whether the

technology is to be actively pursued, and in what direction it will be taken. For example, a higher payload requirement could drive the size of the vehicle upwards, to the point where Shuttle launch would no longer be possible, and the TAV would operate exclusively in the low-orbit and suborbital regime. Through the application of hybrid ramjet/rocket technology, it might even be possible to create a TAV that could launch itself from a normal runway, provided that the inevitably greater time, risk and cost could be accepted in the development stage; such a vehicle would not be for the year 2000.

It is, however, probable that some form of small re-usable spacecraft or TAV will appear before the end of the century. Boeing's ALSV study showed that a workable vehicle could be developed using a high proportion of existing components, and tested within six years of a decision to go-ahead.

The TAV or small spacecraft would be a very significant part of the increased military presence in space in the year 2000, giving the military a monopoly of the most convenient access to space, and the highest mobility outside the atmosphere. This will be important, as space becomes the base and testing ground for a new generation of strategic systems.

STARWARS

What has become popularly known in the USA as the 'Star Wars' defence plan presents a problem for the futurologist. It could be the most significant advance in military technology

Commercial exploitation of space could progress in a number of dramatic directions. The huge celestial umbrella (left) is an array of solar cells acting as a flying power station to support long endurance Shuttle Flights. Above is a potential application, a mining site on the moon with workers 'housed' in two discarded Shuttle external tanks while robots mine for Ilmentite - a step towards the production of liquid oxygen to be shipped up to an orbiting lunar way-station by the lander vehicle at top right. Space is an ideal environment for robots with zero or lunar gravity reducing mechanical workloads although some human intervention would be necessary since the advent of the ICBM itself. At the other extreme, the entire programme could be cancelled at the committee stage within a few months of this book's appearance. However, an account of the stage that the development had reached by the end of 1983 shows the potential of the new technologies involved; their development will continue, even if the current master plan does not.

The basic principle of a ballistic missile defence system is 'layered defence'. Hostile ballistic missiles are attacked by a succession of different weapons as they proceed towards their targets. Each line of defence is designed to let through only ten per cent of the missiles which encounter it, so that only one re-entry vehicle (RV) reaches its target for every thousand launched. This is not just desirable, but essential; unless a high proportion of attacking RVs can be killed, the entire system can be circumvented by simply building more missiles, each carrying greater numbers of RVs. Strategically, the whole purpose of such a system is to make the continued proliferation of ICBMs unattractive.

ICBMs can be launched in surges. If the defensive system is to be able to function at all, it must be able to engage ICBMs, and their payloads of RVs, throughout their flights, and at a considerable rate. Ground-based systems alone are quite inadequate, because they can only engage RVs in the last stages of an attack. Conventional missiles alone are insufficiently accurate, and their limited speed ties up guidance and tracking systems for so long that the necessary high engagement rates cannot be attained.

The solution now under study is to use unconventional weapons, with high velocities and high rates of fire, installed on orbiting platforms. US researchers are looking at lasers (high-energy beams of amplified light) and particle beams, which are based on the same principle as experimental linear accelerators. Lasers transfer heat to the target, while particle beams strike it with a stream of electrons; both have 'muzzle velocities' equal to the speed of light (186 000 miles per second). In addition to these 'directed energy' weapons, US researchers are evaluating the 'electromagnetic railgun'. This uses the same principle as a linear electric motor to accelerate projectiles to speeds of 50 000 mph, and could fire one shot per second.

The first line of defence would comprise massive chemical lasers or electromagnetic railguns, carried by 100-ton satellites orbiting between 500 and 1000 miles above the earth. Their primary mission would be to destroy the missile boosters before the warhead 'buses' could separate and begin to deploy their RVs; the ability to destroy a large percentage of the missiles at this stage is crucial, because the number of targets will increase by a factor of ten or more after RV deployment.

Further layers of defence would be provided by a variety of lasers and particle weapons; X-ray lasers and ground-based lasers aimed by orbiting reflectors are among the concepts under study. Final stages of defence would be provided by infra-red homing interceptor missiles with fragmentation warheads.

Using a number of different weapons is an end in itself, ensuring that any countermeasure will only affect part of the overall defensive system. The system would likewise use a variety of sensors to detect and track ICBMs and RVs; millimetre-wave radar, laser radar and infra-red devices are among them. Engagements would be controlled from supercomputer-equipped battle-management satellites in geostationary orbit. Supercomputer technology is an essential part of the programme, because of the unbelievable precision needed to hit ICBMs with beams or unguided projectiles.

The cost of building such a system cannot be accurately estimated until the technologies have been demonstrated, and that phase alone is expected to cost $21 000 million by 1989–90. An operational system would include multiple satellites of each type, including the biggest chemical lasers and railguns, so that sufficient weapons and back-up vehicles are always in station above hostile launch sites. (It should be noted that the weapon-carrying satellites are not geostationary, so a number of complete batteries would be needed.) It would have to include defensive missiles and other weapons, to protect the system against suppression. A specialised space transportation system, and possibly permanent space stations, would have to be developed to keep the system operational. Even so, its operating costs alone, given the complexity of the system, the manpower to be maintained in orbit, and the frequency of flights and spacewalks or EVAs (extravehicular activity) needed to perform routine maintenance, would be several times the current annual cost of the entire US space programme. A new giant expendable launcher, in the Saturn V/G-1 class, would be needed to launch the largest satellites. The ultimate decision on the programme may be taken on the grounds of economics as much as technology.

DIRECTED ENERGY WEAPONS

Some US intelligence analysts are concerned that the Soviet Union may deploy an experimental charged-particle weapon in space around the end of the 1980s, using a G-1 booster. Such a device will be spectacular, but it will be of very little practical use outside a co-ordinated system, and this will be as difficult for the Soviet Union to field as for the United States. It simply illustrates the fundamental problems with space-based strategic weapons: that they as manoeuvrable as a concrete silo, as hard as a light-alloy bomber, and as stealthy as a small planet.

Lasers, particle weapons and railguns might be more likely to take part in the tactical war in space, in which the key elements will be securing one's own spaceborne C3I (command, communications, control and intelligence) while attempting to disable, destroy or confuse the opposition's. C3I embraces all the current military uses of space, and the most likely future roles for military orbital systems, including TAVs.

Strategic reconnaissance, and the collection of signals intelligence, are largely the work of satellites. One major improvement in this area, on which work is almost certainly proceeding in deepest secrecy, is the Stealth satellite. The primary drawback of the conventional reconnaissance satellite is that the subject is well aware that he is observed, and satellite intelligence has to be carefully filtered for disinformation and deception. A reduced-observables reconnaissance satellite would probably be launched 'piggy-back' style from a non-covert space vehicle, so as not to give clues to its existence, and could open up some valuable sources of information.

Another development in the same general area is the use of

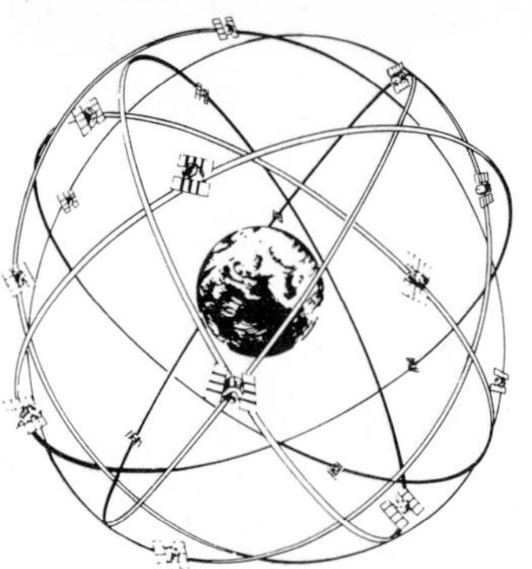

The Navstar Global Positioning System (GPS) is designed to give a series of artificial reference points in space to allow terrestial navigators to fix their position with extreme accuracy. There will be at least 18 satellites in the operational military Navstar system positioned in six orbital planes, 11,000 nautical miles above the earth

satellites for near-real-time surveillance. An example is a US project named Teal Ruby, aimed at tracking aircraft in flight with an orbital infra-red sensor; another is a Soviet satellite type in the Cosmos series, which is apparently designed to track US carrier battle groups. The latter illustrates one of the issues involved in surveillance satellites; active detection systems, such as the radar system carried by the Cosmos type, use rather more power than conventional solar arrays can supply. Cosmos 954, one of this family, caused something of a stir in the late 1970s when it decayed from orbit and its nuclear powerplant landed in small fragments on Canada.

Other satellites will be used for communications and navigation; 'customers' of the US Navstar/Global Positioning System (GPS) will include ships, aircraft and even army groups using a small portable terminal. Some designers of unmanned aircraft are working on even smaller GPS terminals for use in reconnaissance drones.

With the increasing military use of satellites will come the increasing deployment of anti-satellite (ASAT) weapons. Both the Soviet Union and the USA have such weapons, which function by placing a cloud of small pellets in the path of another satellite. The inertia of the pellets, together with the speed of the satellite, is enough to disable the target. Some ASATs take the form of manoeuvrable satellites, which can be placed in orbit until they are directed against a target (the Soviet weapon falls into this class) others are 'direct ascent' weapons like the US ASAT, which is fired from an F-15. There is not a great deal that can be done to protect satellites from this sort of attack. Adding manoeuvring capability virtually eliminates the payload because of the amount of fuel required, and only the largest vehicles will be able to mount useful defensive weapons. The vulnerability of conventional satellites may be a potent argument in favour of the TAV.

There are few military uses of space, apart from the controversial strategic defence plan, that call for the constant presence of a human operator, and advances in VHSIC and artificial intelligence will probably keep pace with most developments. The same is true of most commercial space applications which may not require human operators.

Of all commercial uses of space, the most important in the year 2000 will almost certainly be the application which is most important today: communications. Space technology has provided the global links for conventional telecommunications, and as these merge with the world of data processing the demand for communications capacity will continue to increase rapidly. As it does so, a problem will have to be solved: some of the key comsat operating locations, in geostationary orbit above the Atlantic and Pacific, will become both electronically and physically overloaded. The answer will be to group functions together in a single co-ordinated package. However, this does not necessarily imply one satellite. Instead, a formation of satellites would orbit close together, linked by extremely-high-frequency radio links or even modulated lasers. Unlike a single large vehicle, such a satellite cluster would not be permanently degraded by a single failure. The affected satellite would be de-orbited with its thrusters, and a replacement launched into the same area.

Space manufacturing is a possible area of development, but depends on the future commercial development of space transportation systems; there must be an economical way of moving relatively small quantities of raw materials and finished products in and out of orbit. Some of the most successful recent experiments with space manufacturing have been in the medical field; apparently, live cells can be separated from cultures in the virtual absence of gravity in a manner which is quite impossible on earth. The development of a commercial/scientific space station might make manufacturing a reasonable proposition by the late 1990s.

With all these different space vehicles aloft, there may arise a need for a new type of satellite, a robotic machine with a large capacity for manoeuvring fuel, a high degree of intelligence, accurate flight control and sensitive passive optical scanners. Its mission would be to rendezvous with inert satellites and discarded casings, and administer a gentle retro-thrust into the pyre of uncontrolled re-entry. It would be a fairly costly device, but after a few billion-dollar collisions the world's space agencies and insurers might find themselves persuaded to invest in an unglamorous but vital system — the Orbital Refuse Cart.

0.4

Military Aircraft

The X-29A takes shape at the Grumman factory

Exotic shapes, new materials, advanced engines and immensely sophisticated systems are among the factors which will transform the fighting aircraft by the year 2000. Behind the change are the recognition that the manned aircraft will continue, indefinitely, to be a vital weapon in all kinds of warfare, and experience of the constantly moving, dynamic and unpredictable air combat arenas of the 1970s.

Perhaps the key change between the present and next generation is that today's aircraft, typified by the US designs which emerged in 1970-74, were designed mainly to fight and win against other aircraft. But three combat experiences, in the Middle East in 1967 and 1973, and over North Vietnam in 1972, demonstrated new threats to airpower, in the shape of saturation salvoes of surface-to-air missiles (SAMs) and intense attacks on the fixed air bases to which most modern combat aircraft are tied. Once the potential of SAMs and counter-air weaponry was recognised, development of new and improved systems gathered pace. As well as dealing with other aircraft, the future combat aircraft will have to survive in the face of SAMs and operate despite anything which may happen to its base.

Geopolitics will also affect the design of new aircraft, particularly tactical combat aircraft and support systems. The turbulence of the 1970s, and the recognition of the world's limited supplies of strategic materials and fuels, has made it plain that an effective military force must be mobile and versatile. Tactical aircraft must be able to reach the battlefield, wherever it may be.

STEALTH

Most of the technology being developed for aircraft such as the Advanced Technology Bomber (ATB), better known as the Stealth bomber, and the Advanced Tactical Fighter (ATF) is aimed at one or other of these survival problems. The ATB is designed to frustrate SAMs and interceptors by being hard to detect and track; the ATF will, in addition, fly fast and high to reduce its exposure to defences. While the long-range ATB is not vulnerable to tactical anti-air-base weapons, the ATF will have short take-off and landing (Stol) characteristics. Navigation and attack systems in both aircraft will improve their chances of survival: an accurate, effective attack on the first pass means that no aircraft need approach the same target twice.

Stealth will be a strong influence on the design of any aircraft intended to face air and missile defences, and the primary design goal for certain types. Its influence on shape can already be seen in advanced fighter studies, and it is also important in the design of many subsystems.

Stealth is a design objective, not a single technical breakthrough, although some new technical features have been specially developed to attain it. It is also referred to as 'reduced observables', a slightly more accurate term. To destroy an aircraft, defensive systems, SAMs or fighters, need to detect it, identify it and track it by the physical signs of its presence: its reflection on a radar screen, emissions from its own electronic systems, its image in an optical tracker, or the heat of its airframe and engines. Technically, these signs are called 'signatures'. Designing an aircraft for stealth means reducing its signatures, by a wide variety of means. Like any design objective, stealth is compatible with some other objectives and conflicts with others, so the designer must arrive at a compromise which is best for the specific mission. It follows that some aircraft will be stealthier than others. Pure reconnaissance aircraft, for example, will be the stealthiest of all, followed by bombers and cruise missiles. The ATF will be less stealthy than these.

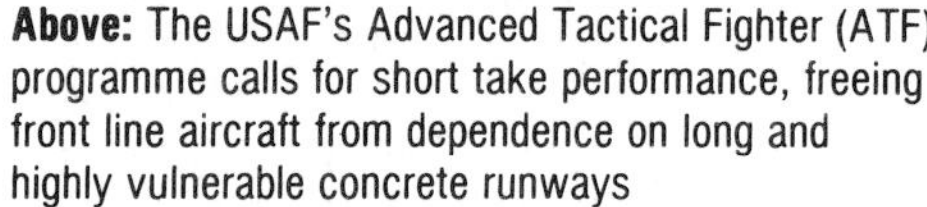

Above: The USAF's Advanced Tactical Fighter (ATF) programme calls for short take performance, freeing front line aircraft from dependence on long and highly vulnerable concrete runways

Design for stealth begins with the defensive systems that are to be outwitted. The most important of these will continue to be radar, because of its sheer range and its ability to penetrate the atmosphere. Two characteristics of radar makes it vulnerable to Stealth countermeasures: it works much better against metal than anything else, and it relies for its effectiveness on peculiarities of the target's shape which focus and amplify the return signal.

Very stealthy aircraft such as the ATB will be the most significant applications of composite materials, which make poor radar reflectors. In addition, though, they will incorporate plastic materials which actually absorb radar waves and dissipate them as an insignificant amount of heat. While these will probably not be used for primary structure, they will be built into crucial areas such as the edges of the wing and control surfaces. The insides of these radar-absorbing structures may resemble the soft plastic wedges which line the walls of electronic test cells to render them electromagnetically 'dead'. A final reduction in reflected energy is achieved by special paints which can diffuse a small amount of radar energy.

The shape of the stealth aircraft is just as important, if not more so. The object of a stealthy configuration is to eliminate good radar reflectors. As most radar waves impinge on the airframe at a near-horizontal angle, vertical and near-vertical surfaces are to be made of minimum size or eliminated. Reentrant corners, such as a conventional wing-fuselage junction, can also generate hot-spots on radar. Wing/body

Another solution to evading hostile surface to air missiles is the 'high-fast' option, the way this Lockheed Mach 8 aircraft might operate

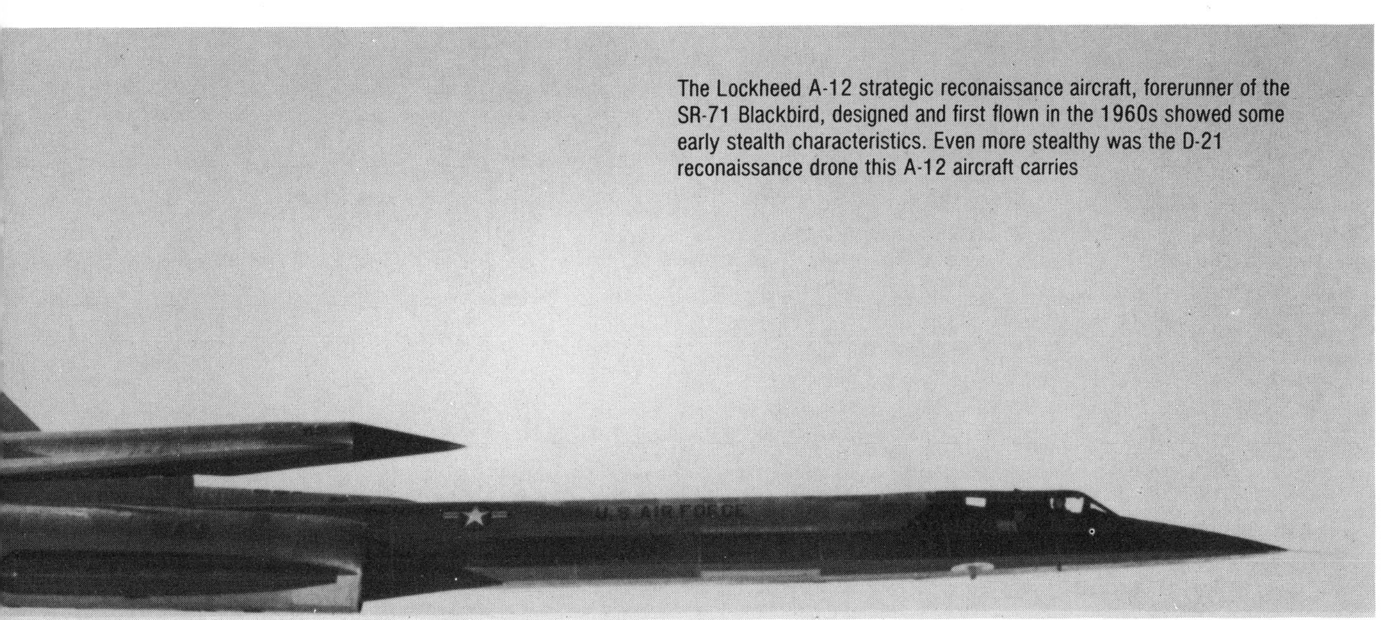

The Lockheed A-12 strategic reconaissance aircraft, forerunner of the SR-71 Blackbird, designed and first flown in the 1960s showed some early stealth characteristics. Even more stealthy was the D-21 reconaissance drone this A-12 aircraft carries

The long-range manned penetrating bomber presents one of the greatest technical challenges facing aircraft designers while performing a deterrent function that some might doubt was still cost-effective. Supporters of the manned bomber say it is the only way to cover mobile targets and has far more operational flexibility than non-recallable strategic missiles. These

USAF proposals of the early 1980s show alternative solutions to the problem, an aircraft (left) with high mounted engines and semi-blended wing/fuselage for optimum stealthiness and an aircraft (right and below) featuring a slewed wing. At low speed the aircraft would fly conventionally while at high speed it would rely on its lifting body fuselage

blending, used on the F-16 and B-1, not only reduces radar image but also dramatically improves efficiency, reducing weight and increasing internal volume with a negligible effect on drag; blended shapes will be standard for all combat aircraft by the year 2000.

Very stealthy aircraft will take blending all the way, until fuselage and wing merge into one. The Northrop ATB is reported to be a flying wing, with crew, weapons, engines and systems housed in a thick swept or delta wing and no fuselage at all. Alternatively, high-stealth designs may develop into lifting-body-type aircraft reminiscent of those tested by NASA in the late 1960s and early 1970s. While the lifting body and the flying wing may seem to be opposites, they are quite similar and are mainly different in aspect ratio. The longer-span flying wing is more suited to long-range aircraft, while lifting-body shapes will be more apparent on low-level high-speed types. Lockheed's F-19, developed to strike high-value, heavily-defended targets, could well be an example of the latter.

Almost as important to stealth as the basic configuration of the aircraft is the engine installation. Classic engine and inlet designs, consisting of a sharp-lipped metal tube with a whirling mass of solid metal at the end, are among the most effective radar reflectors on many conventional aircraft, while the strongest infra-red signals come out of the rear end of the engine. In the ATB and F-19, the engines are probably buried in long, curved tunnels with absorbent walls, at some considerable cost in efficiency; the tunnels represent a great deal of wasted volume in the airframe. Streamwise baffles can be installed to block the radar's view of the engine completely, as on the B-1B. The engine might exhaust through a 'conformal' nozzle, designed to protect the hot metal of the rear turbine stages from detection; slatted 'Venetian blind' exhaust shields have also been considered.

Successful stealth design demands that all the aircraft's signatures are reduced simultaneously. Stealth aircraft will incorporate noise-absorbing material and size and visibility to electro-optical systems such as missile trackers will be reduced. One intriguing technique is 'active camouflage': a system of lights on the underside of the aircraft, coupled to sensors on its upper surface, which illuminate the wings and belly to match exactly the illumination from the sky. While an aircraft using this technique would not be invisible to the naked eye, it might well fool the less refined circuits of an electro-optical tracker.

Advanced electronics make a great contribution to stealth. Fly-by-wire or fly-by-light control systems will make manageable flying machines out of the most exotic configurations, and will allow control surfaces such as fins and rudders to be reduced in size, or even eliminated as on the Northrop ATB. Better radar processing will mean that aircraft like the ATB will be able to find their targets or hug the ground under automatic control, while using much less raw radar power than previous systems.

Even the stealthiest aircraft are by no means invisible, but stealth presents the attacker with opportunities, and poses problems for the defences. A SAM system designed to cope with a normal aircraft, for example, might be rendered useless against a target with a much smaller radar image. Eventually, the target would approach close enough for the radar to detect it, but by that time it might be inside the minimum range of the system's missiles. At some considerable cost in both complexity and mobility, the power of the radar could be increased to cope with the stealthy attackers. But this raises the question of whether the system needs to cope with the worst case (a highly stealthy configuration such as the F-19) or with less stealthy aircraft. Either way, the increased power of the system makes it more susceptible to location by an intruder's passive electronic surveillance equipment.

ELECTRONIC COUNTERMEASURES

Another operational aspect of stealth is its relationship to the electronic countermeasures (ECM) carried by the aircraft. If the aircraft has a small radar image, it takes much less power to mask that image by jamming, or to generate a convincing false image through deception techniques. The task of the ECM suite immediately becomes much easier. What is more, there are many ECM techniques which will work with a small target, but not with a large one. Combined with the lower power requirement, this gives the attacker a wider range of tactics, while the defender has to eliminate a far wider range of ECM possibilities before he can tell a genuine target from deception.

Stealth, in short, is a way of intensifying the 'fog of battle', the confusion and lack of clear, immediate and total vision which distinguishes military action from military history. The elegance of the concept, though, is that it thickens the fog for the defenders only, not for the attacker.

If stealth were a miracle breakthrough with no performance penalties whatsoever, it would be applied without delay to every combat aircraft in service. But stealth is, as noted earlier, a design objective, and, at the levels of reduced observability planned for the ATB and F-19, is a highly sensitive attribute. It is probably correct to say that an aircraft is as stealthy as its most prominent signature, in whatever spectrum and at whatever bearing. Other performance and operational aspects must be subordinated to suppressing any 'spikes' on the signature charts.

This Grumman proposal shows pronounced stealth characteristics - blended wing/body form, high mounted engine intake and hot exhaust screening

To begin with, design for efficient supersonic flight is apparently incompatible with very stealthy design. Engines will not function efficiently or consistently at very high speeds behind a curved, baffled, blunt-lipped inlet, or with a shrouded exhaust system. Combining extreme stealth with high agility is also difficult, since highly manoeuvrable aircraft, even with advanced control systems, need large and powerful control surfaces in relation to their size and, once again, straightforward inlets to optimise engine performance over a broad range of speeds, attitudes and altitudes.

For the designer of everyday tactical combat aircraft, stealth has one critical drawback; it is highly compromised by externally-mounted weapons or fuel tanks. For an unarmed reconnaissance aircraft or a dedicated strategic bomber, this is not a serious problem. The tactical fighter, by contrast, has no alternative to external weapon carriage. Internal weapon bays are immensely costly in terms of airframe size and

weight. With current and contemplated technology, there is no alternative at all to external carriage for air-to-air or air-to-surface missiles. Above all, the tactical fighter design has to provide for weapons as yet unconceived. For this reason, if for no other, future tactical combat aircraft will not be able to entrust their survival primarily to stealth.

By the year 2000, two roles should be filled by dedicated stealth designs, strategic bombing and reconnaissance. In the latter role, the Lockheed F-19 is already in service, while a Northrop-led team including Boeing and Vought is working on development of the ATB, which is to enter service in the first half of the 1990s. By the year 2000, Strategic Air Command should have all its 110 ATBs in service. Given the longevity of previous Lockheed types, it is likely that derivatives of the F-19 will remain in service, and possibly in production.

Both the ATB and the F-19 have been wrapped in tighter secrecy than any previous programmes; one of the many sensitive aspects of stealth is that the external shape of the aircraft is too important an element of the technology to be casually revealed. It is, however, possible to give a brief account of some of the technology and philosophy behind the ATB, which is likely to be a crucial military asset in the year 2000.

The Northrop ATB will be somewhat smaller than the B-1. The B-1B is bigger and heavier partly because the basic design is older, and was designed to carry multiple decoys and AGM-69 missiles to supress defences, and partly because it is now intended to carry cruise missiles or even conventional weapons, which have much less destructive power per pound of warload lifted. By assigning these growth and second-line roles to the B-1, the USAF has been able to keep the size of the ATB down.

The other immediate distinguishing mark of the ATB is that it is a bodiless 'flying wing' design. Not only is this configuration very stealthy, with no vertical angles and extremely slender side and front elevations, but it is also extremely efficient. The weight of the aircraft is distributed smoothly along the span of the wing, rather than being concentrated at its centre, so that the wing structure is less highly loaded and can be lighter. The drag of the fuselage and tail surfaces is eliminated.

FLYING WINGS

Flying wings have been built and flown before, the biggest of them by Northrop, and one just retired bomber, the British Aerospace Vulcan, is very close to a flying-wing configuration. Like canard-type aircraft, though, they have made relatively little headway against conventional configurations with large wing flaps and familiar stability and control characteristics. The ability of electronically signalled controls to make unstable configurations flyable reduces the penalties affecting flying-wing designs. Rockwell studies of an advanced flying wing bomber showed that its structure might account for only 13 per cent of its take-off weight, compared with 20 per cent for a conventional aircraft using the same technology; Boeing investigations of a giant flying-wing freighter showed that it could carry half its maximum weight in payload, compared with less than 30 per cent for a 747. Using a flying wing for a stealth bomber is 'synergistic', as systems analysts would put it, because the efficiency of the configuration makes it possible to accomplish the mission with a lighter, smaller aircraft, which by its very nature is harder to detect.

While a flying wing would have naturally poor low-level, high-speed characteristics, giving its crew an unacceptably rough ride and placing heavy loads on its structure, mission-adaptive wing (MAW) technology, which is currently being developed and tested by ATB team-member Boeing, could be used to provide artificially good gust response. The absence of control-surface gaps in the skin could also contribute to a

Stealth proposals are highly reminiscent of the flying wings fashionable in the late '40s and exemplified by Northrop's extraordinary YB-49 killed off by government indifference and by the fact it could not carry the bulky atomic weapons of the period. The Grumman strike aircraft proposal (above) gets close to a flying wing but in fact the US Air Force never quite let go. The sci-fi shapes (left) actually date from the mid 1950s

lower radar image at some angles.

Subtlety and silence will be the main requirements for the ATB's electronic systems. A common technology in many of these is advanced signal processing, that is, computer hardware and programs designed to apply sophisticated mathematical analysis techniques to incoming signals. High-speed signal processors, possibly using VHSIC techniques, will extract necessary information from short, low-power radar transmissions, and improve the quality of passive, non-emitting systems such as forward-looking infra-red (FLIR) scanners. Very powerful processors will also be used in the electronic warfare (EW) suite, locating and analysing enemy radars, judging whether the aircraft is in danger of detection and deploying the many jamming and deception devices.

The existence and potential of the ATB shows that reports of the manned bomber's death have, once again, been exaggerated. The Advanced Tactical Fighter, by contrast, is two generations into the rediscovery of air-to-air combat. It represents an intriguing mixture of concepts, some returned from a long exile, some completely new and some carried over from the present generation.

Given the inability of stealth to provide complete protection for a tactical combat aircraft, one of the main aims in defining basic ATF requirements, a process which started in the late 1970s, was to find a way of defeating dense SAM defences. Tactical SAM systems have come a long way in the past decade, particularly in the Soviet Union which has devised a complete defensive net for its forces based on a whole range

of missile systems. Together with the increasing use of fighters armed with look-down, shoot-down radar/missile systems, this missile armoury is making low-level, under-the-radar operations increasingly difficult.

ATF will head in the other direction, into what is called the 'high, fast sanctuary'. Very little attention was paid to survival through high speed and altitude between the 1960s, when the accepted doctrine was that high-altitude aircraft would be easy targets for SAMs, and the late 1970s. The doctrine was too simple a dismissal of a complex case, as has been shown by the thousands of unwelcome overflights carried out by Lockheed A-12s and SR-71s since 1964, without a single loss to hostile action.

Flying at sustained supersonic speed and high altitude, first of all, eliminates all but the biggest and most costly mobile tactical missiles. Stealth technology, which was applied to the A-12 and SR-71 in much the same degree as it could be applied to ATF, serves to reduce warning time for the defences or, if the radar power is increased, gives the intruder more warning of an operating missile site. In addition, ATF will be designed to manoeuvre at supersonic speed.

This poses a problem for missile designers. Most missiles are propelled by solid rockets which burn for only the first few seconds of flight, leaving the weapon to coast. To reduce drag in the thick air of lower altitudes, so that the motor can accelerate the missile to maximum speed, rocket-driven SAMs must have small wings. Once a missile reaches high altitude, any turning manoeuvre is aerodynamically inefficient and eats into the missile's finite store of kinetic energy. If a supersonic target pulls a modestly tight turn after the missile has ascended into the stratosphere, the SAM may run out of manoeuvring energy, or 'go ballistic'.

There are no easy answers for the defenders. Bigger missiles can be built, but cannot be integrated into a realistically sized mobile system. Covering a large area with fixed sites is expensive, and fixed heavy missile sites are tempting targets, of high value and considerable vulnerability.

What has made the 'high, fast' option more attractive for ATF is that such performance can now be built into a more affordable aircraft. Evading missile defences requires sustained supersonic, high-altitude performance, but current fighters need to use afterburning to attain supersonic speed, and have little supersonic endurance. ATF should be much more efficient at supersonic speed, for a number of reasons.

The development of better configurations for supersonic cruise, aided by advanced automatic flight control systems, is an important factor. The most aerodynamically advanced experimental fighter flown to date, General Dynamics' F-16XL, points the way to some of these new shapes. Its cranked-arrow wing has many of the advantages of the slender delta, an idealised supersonic configuration; it allows a long, slim airframe without excessive weight, much of the wing falls behind the primary shock-wave from the nose and it

Aircraft designed in the 1970s for service in the 1980s are being redesigned and put back into production with new avionics or weapon systems and will be around in large numbers well into the next century. France's Mirage 4000 (far left) clearly derives from the thirty year line of Dassault deltas yet is an air superiority and strike fighter of world class performance. The F-15 Eagle meanwhile has been developed into a penetrating strike aircraft with a large weapons load (above) and has been selected as the USAF's derivative fighter. Beyond the dual-role fighter is the ATF proper which has engendered ambitious proposals from major US manufacturers (below).

provides tremendous carrying space for weapons. But the plain delta has disadvantages too. Its pitch controls are close to the centre of gravity, and must therefore produce a strong downforce (trim drag) to balance the aircraft. Its span is short, so it is inefficient at low speeds or in a turn, and its manoeuvrability is hampered further by the fact that the short trailing edge has to provide both pitch and roll control.

The cranked-arrow wing of the F-16XL is, in a sense, two wings in one. The inner section is a highly swept, deep and capacious slender delta, while the outer section is a thin-section, sharp-lipped wing of moderate sweep. Trim drag is reduced by moving the centre of gravity aft of the centre of lift, taming the flying characteristics with the automatic flight control system. Not only is there a greater length of trailing edge available for pitch and roll control, but the leading-edge flaps on the outer wing are, uniquely, also used for augmented roll control. The F-16XL pitches and rolls faster than the basic F-16.

The F-16XL also uses a concept called 'vortex lift'. At moderate to high angles of attack, the junctions between the wing and the fuselage, and between the inner and outer wings, generate high-energy, swirling vortices. As these stream back over the wing, they actually stabilise airflow, reduce pressures above the wing and increase the ratio of lift to drag. Currently, vortex lift is one of the black arts of aerodynamics, being hard to predict or simulate, but this may prove to be one of the most rewarding areas of research for new aerodynamic simulation computers in the next few years.

The XL itself is not a supersonic-cruise aircraft; it was originally designed as such, but was modified to reflect air force requirements for a high-subsonic-speed strike aircraft with improved range and efficiency. It nonetheless includes many features which any ATF proposal will have to copy or match in order to meet the USAF's needs.

Modified deltas are not the only way to achieve supersonic cruise. McDonnell Douglas has shown at least one design with unswept, medium-aspect-ratio wings of very thin section. Aerodynamically, this is an excellent solution; structurally, the combination of high loads, long span and thin section is impossible by conventional means. Variable-camber mission-adaptive-wing techniques, though, would be used to dump lift

Left: One hundred B-1B strategic bombers will begin entering USAF service in the mid 1980s when they will take over the manned penetrating bomber role from the venerable B-52's of Strategic Air Command. By the year 2000, on present plans, the advanced technology bomber will have assumed the penetrating role, in turn relegating the B-1B to long range conventional roles and cruise missile carrying. The B-1 design dates back to the early 1970s but its blended wing form shows some stealth characteristics

Below: The General Dynamics F-16XL was the unsuccessful contender in 1984 for the USAF's derivative fighter requirement. The cranked arrow wing is aerodynamically efficient at supersonic speed and also in the high subsonic speed strike role demanded by the air force while offering the advantage of tremendous carrying space for underwing weapons and internal fuel tankage

from the outer wings under high load, reducing the peak bending moment on the spar and bringing the structural loads back within reason. Aeroelastic tailoring will also lift some constraints from basic design, and, combined with MAW, could lead to some unexpectedly slender sweptback or swept-forward wing shapes for ATF studies.

SUPERCRUISE

As well as achieving supersonic cruise, the eventual ATF configuration will also be designed for high agility and short-field performance. Manoevrability requirements are another point of contact between the F-16XL and the ATF. The original F-16 and the F-15 were designed for close-quarters air-to-air combat, using the weapons and avionics available at the time of their conception. In-service versions of the Sidewinder air-to-air missile (AAM) at that time were most likely to score a kill if fired from inside a space described by a cone, centred on the target's tail, while radar-assisted gunsight technology defined a similar but smaller gun-firing envelope. As a result, air combats often became turning contests as the protagonists tried to protect their own tails or manoeuvre into an enemy's cone, and the ability to sustain a high-g turn, at a constant speed and altitude, became the most important factor in combat aircraft design.

No sooner were the new types in service than a single weapon brought a tremendous change to the picture: the AIM-9L Sidewinder AAM. The AIM-9L has a drastically improved kill probability, whether fired head-on or at any other aspect. No longer does the fighter pilot need to hang leech-like on his opponent's tail; if he can slew his aircraft on to any target within range, at any angle, he has a good chance

Left: The USAF's AFTI (Advanced Fighter Technology Integrator) which can use its digital flight control system to fly unlike any other combat aircraft

Above: The 'all-aspect' capable AIM-9L Sidewinder air to air missile - to exploit weapons such as these, the AFTI programme is exploring 'instaneous manoeuvre'

of a kill if he can hold it long enough for the missile to fire and guide. Losing speed or altitude in the process is relatively unimportant if the kill has been achieved. Indefinitely sustained manoeuvre becomes less important than the 'instantaneous manoeuvre' capability of the aircraft, that is, the maximum rate at which it can be manoeuvred at a given speed. New gun-aiming technology demonstrated by the Firefly/IFFC programme (see Chapter 2) will extend the same considerations to the fighter's other short-range weapon.

The F-16XL's powerful controls give it better instantaneous manoeuvre than the basic F-16, while the standard aircraft is better in a sustained turn. The ATF can be expected to continue this trend, but will add to it the sort of technology being developed on another modified Fighting Falcon, the Advanced Fighter Technology Integrator (AFTI)/F-16. This aircraft flew in 1982, equipped with a Bendix digital flight control system (DFCS) and two large all-moving fins beneath the air intake, canted out and down at a 45-degree angle. Using the conventional control surfaces, manoeuvring flaps and the new fins under the control of the DFCS, the AFTI/F-16 can fly unlike any previous aircraft. When a normal aircraft changes direction, it also changes its attitude; to change heading, for example, the fuselage turns to the new heading and the wings bank into the turn. Flightpath and attitude are said to be 'coupled'. But the AFTI/F-16 control system generates new options. For example, as the elevators and manoeuvring flaps drive the aircraft upwards, the forward fins can move to cancel out the usual pitching moment, so the aircraft can rise or descend in a constant attitude. Conversely, the aeroplane can pitch without changing its flightpath. This 'decoupled' control also works in the yaw axis, so that the fighter can 'crab' without turning or banking, or slew its fuselage around without changing direction unlike conventional aircraft.

Decoupled control has some very interesting implications for weapons delivery. In air-to-air combat, it gives the pilot a number of new ways of bringing his gun to bear on a target almost instantaneously; combined with IFFC techniques, the gun could become a very lethal weapon. But the AFTI/F-16 is also being tested for the ground-attack role, with the DFCS coupled to an electro-optical tracking and ranging device. As with the IFFC equipment, the idea is that the pilot keeps the tracking grid in the head-up display over the target. The FLIR (forward-looking infra-red) system provides accurate tracking, the laser provides range information, and the DFCS makes precise, decoupled aircraft movements so that the bomb is released on exactly the right trajectory.

These tests fall firmly into the high-risk bracket, because they involve low-level diving bomb runs in which the pilot is not directly connected to the controls, he is simply issuing his commands to the DFCS, which is flying the aircraft according to target data. The payoff is also high. The objective is to release a simple bomb at 200 feet and 590 knots, a mile away from the target, and get the same accuracy as with a guided weapon. The bomb is cheap, plentiful in wartime and impossible to jam, and requires no further help from the launch aircraft. If the system works, it will lead to a reassessment of the value of the bomb and the need for short-range missiles.

Uncoupled manoeuvre will almost certainly be featured by ATF, and will probably drive the designers towards a canard configuration. Apart from supersonic cruise and manoeuvre, though, ATF configurations will need to meet another new requirement: short take-off and landing (Stol) performance.

DOING WITHOUT RUNWAYS

Most current combat aircraft are designed to use two-mile, hard-concrete runways, and suffer increasing performance penalties as the runway length available is reduced. The vulnerability of the runway is at last being appreciated; the countermeasure proposed by ATF planners is to provide for operations from damaged airfields. This will certainly mean operating from shorter field lengths. While it only takes a few hits to put an airfield's two-mile runways out of action, it is much more difficult to eliminate every straight 1500-foot section, and it is much easier to repair an airfield to that level.

Five hundred yards, or under one-sixth of the length of the standard Nato runway, is the field-length goal for the ATF. This is not quite as demanding as it sounds. Current fighters already have two of the elements needed for Stol operations: high thrust/weight ratio and low wing loading. They still need long runways, for a number of reasons. When an F-16 takes off, it has to accelerate until its tailplane can produce enough downforce to 'rotate' the aircraft, lifting the nose and allowing the wing to generate lift. If this 'rotation speed' could be reduced, the aircraft could take off at a much lower speed. On landing, one problem is that wheelbrakes are limited in effectiveness, particularly when allowances must be made for wet or icy runways. Another is that a jet fighter's control response on approach is seldom good. The engine is large in proportion to the aircraft, and takes time to accelerate and decelerate. If the pilot finds himself above the glideslope, the flightpath to

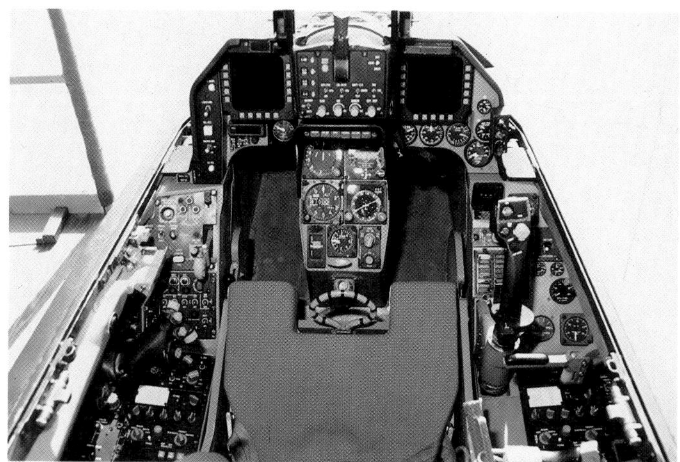

Above: The AFTI/F-16's cockpit with multi function displays and a large Marconi Avionics HUD. The aircraft has been tested with digital flight control and target seekers coupled for superaccurate weapon delivery

Right: The very long concrete runways on which contemporary combat aircraft depend would be the first targets of any future 'counterair' war. A five hundred yard takeoff is the requirement for the USAF's advanced tactical fighter with unhindered performance in conventional flight. The USAF's solution is a vectoring and reversing engine nozzle, which would operate in all flight regimes, on take off and during manoeuvering as shown in these ATF proposals. The US Navy meanwhile is developing similar concepts (below)

the end of the runway, and drops the nose to reduce lift, the fighter will accelerate away from the glideslope before the engine responds to the throttle. In operational service, this means that the landing field length has to include a 'scatter margin' to allow for the fact that most landings will miss the exact end of the runway.

The US Air Force's solution for all these problems is a single device: a vectoring and reversing engine nozzle. While neither reversing nor vectoring is new, the combination of the two is innovative, as is the use which the USAF plans to make of it. The new nozzle will be able to reverse all or part of the engine's unreheated thrust, on the ground or in flight, and vector the full thrust of the engine some 30 degrees upwards or downwards. It will also be variable in area and internal profile to match speed and thrust, like the exhaust nozzles of current aircraft. Because a conventional circular nozzle incorporating all these features would be a mechanical nightmare, the new nozzle will be rectangular in cross-section, with fixed sidewalls forming the short sides. Two sets of doors and cascades make up the long sides, and because they all move in the same plane the nozzle is described as a 'two-dimensional' or 2-D design.

The 2-D nozzle will be an integral part of the ATF and of its engine. It will be controlled by the engine's digital electronic engine control (DEEC) which is turn will co-operate with the digital flight control system. The nozzle will get its orders from the pilot either through the throttle lever and the DEEC, or through the flight controls via the DFCS; as far as the pilot is concerned, the nozzle will be fully automatic.

The nozzle will operate at all times. The ATF will start its

take-off roll with the throttle open, and the nozzle pointed aft, for maximum acceleration. At rotation speed, which will be a good deal slower than that of current aircraft, the pilot will pull back on the stick, and the DFCS and DEEC will deflect the nozzle upwards to force the nose up. Deflecting engine thrust upwards on take-off may seem odd, but a high-powered fighter has enough lift and power to get away with it.

In flight, the 2-D nozzle will provide added pitch control power for manoeuvring, particularly in what is called 'the upper left-hand corner'. This expression, derived from the shape of the standard performance chart, refers to flight at low airspeeds and high altitudes, when aerodynamic controls are least effective. By very small adjustments of the nozzle angle, too, the 2-D system can provide zero-drag trim to balance the aircraft, and the in-flight reversing system provides rapid deceleration. The last-mentioned attribute could be a useful combat manoeuvre, because, unlike an airbrake, it gives a pursuer no visual 'cues' and could cause him to overshoot.

On landing, the 2-D nozzle's ability to reverse part or all of the exhaust, combined with movable cascades in the reverser ducts, will give the ATF pilot responsive, precise and decoupled control over his forward speed. The vectoring facility could also be used as for pitch control, giving a canard ATF the advantages of a three-surface layout. Accurate control means accurate touchdowns, followed by a landing roll using full reverse thrust.

The 2-D nozzle is heavier than a conventional design. A nozzle, after all, is a pressure vessel, and is most efficient when it is circular. However, it can reduce drag in cruising flight, saving fuel; it allows the use of a smaller, lighter tail or foreplane and eliminates the need for an airbrake.

The ATF's engines themselves are likely to mark a substantial step forward in basic gas-turbine technology, as described in Chapter 1; while producing about the same power as current large fighter engines, they will be hundreds of pounds lighter, much simpler and more ruggedly built. They will be very different in other ways, largely because the ATF is designed for sustained flight at supersonic speeds.

Current fighter engines are turbofans, in which about 40 per cent of the airflow bypasses the high-pressure compressor, combustor and turbine and flows directly into the afterburner. Without afterburning (also called reheat or augmentation) the engine moves a relatively large mass of air, at a speed close to the optimum for high-subsonic flight. At higher speeds, though, the engine rapidly becomes less efficient, because the bypassed 'cold' air is moving little faster than the aircraft and produces very little thrust. Even the best of present combat turbofans, the as yet experimental Pratt & Whitney PW1128, runs out of thrust just above Mach 1·2 without afterburning. Reheat increases the temperature and pressure of the exhaust, and the variable nozzle changes shape to allow the higher-pressure stream to expand and escape at much higher speed, for supersonic flight. However, the fuel consumption of the afterburner is so high that its operational use must be measured in minutes.

The ATF engine will probably be more like a turbojet than a turbofan, with less than 20 per cent of the air bypassing the combustor; the amount of reheat boost required will set the exact figure, and the purpose of the bypass system will be to feed the afterburner with cool air and oxygen. Even without the augmentor in operation, the exhaust will be hot and pressurised enough to drive the aircraft at Mach 1·5 to 1·8. Combined with the efficient supersonic configuration, this will provide the sustained supersonic capability that the military requires.

This advanced Tactical Fighter proposal comes from Grumman. The military requirement for sustained supersonic operation, short field performance plus uncoupled manoeuvre presents huge challenges

SUPERCRUISE POWERPLANTS

Designing an engine with the necessary pressure ratio for supercruise is not much more difficult than designing a turbofan, where high core pressures are needed to drive the fan. In many ways, the pure jet is simpler; it is less prone to pressure pulses in the bypass duct, it needs no heavy, fat shaft running from the low-pressure turbine in the back to the fan in the front, and the augmentor lights more reliably and tends to burn more consistently in the hotter airstream. But there is one big problem: heat. While the ratios of pressure and temperature are within today's experience, the absolute temperatures attained within the engine are not. This is a factor of the aircraft's speed. In any jet engine installation, the air entering the intake tends to create drag as it hits the face of the engine and is forcibly slowed down (relative to the engine, that is; in relation to the free air outside, it is accelerating). Normally, this drag is offset by the fact that the air is compressed as it slows down, supercharging the engine and boosting its thrust; this is known as 'ram recovery' and is the basis for efficient air intake design. At high Mach numbers, though, the pressure rise associated with ram recovery becomes extreme, and brings with it a high temperature rise. This is multiplied by the engine pressure ratio, and the result is that temperatures at the back of the engine, downstream of the compressor, rise very rapidly with increasing Mach numbers.

US Navy V/STOL proposal. As well as being a weapons platform of great capability, the aircraft would carry advanced precision guided air to surface munitions and fire and forget air to air missiles

Once they reach the maximum permissible levels, the only answer is to throttle the engine back. This cuts temperatures, but simultaneously reduces the thrust and efficiency of the engine.

The use of sophisticated cooling techniques and new materials in the combustor, turbine and afterburner of future engines will not eliminate the problem, but will postpone its worst effects to higher Mach numbers. Future military engines may have combustors made of carbon-carbon materials, almost impervious to heat, if the problem of protecting them from combustion can be overcome. Some components may be made up of layers of perforated metal, so that cooling air can be distributed evenly through and over a combustor wall or turbine vane. (Exactly analogous to human or animal cooling mechanisms, this is known as 'transpiration cooling'.) Advanced blade aerodynamics will be used in the turbine discs, with the aim of getting equal or better efficiency out of fewer, thicker and shorter blades which can be more easily plumbed with complex internal cooling passages.

Complex 'variable-cycle' engines, which can change from turbofans to turbojets with the aid of internal valves, are probably not on the cards for the ATF. A simpler system, the variable area bypass injector (VABI) might bring an overall benefit, however. It consists of a variable-area nozzle, similar to today's exhaust nozzle, installed between the turbine and augmentor, so that it can expand the exit throat of the core at the expense of the bypass duct, or vice versa. By slight changes in bypass ratio, it is claimed, the VABI can improve transonic and supersonic thrust and reduce subsonic fuel consumption.

Improved supersonic performance demands a change in another aspect of military aircraft design: the way in which a fighter carries weapons. Two current aircraft, the B-1B and the F-16XL, point the way to ATF. The XL, in particular, marks a quantum jump in the efficiency with which a tactical fighter carries its 'disposable load' of fuel and weapons. Thanks to its deep, large-area wing, its internal fuel capacity is 82 per cent greater than that of the standard F-16. More significantly, perhaps, it is 94 per cent of the internal fuel load of the F-15C, which has exactly twice as much installed power to feed. The ATF, too, will need a large internal fuel load, because it is prohibitively inefficient to go supersonic with external fuel tanks.

Under the large-area wing of the XL are troughs for semi-recessed AIM-120 air-to-air missiles (these are no novelty, having been invented for the F-4 in the mid-1950s, but will be standard on future combat aircraft) and simple attachments for bombs and missiles. While the drag of the individual bombs and missiles is the same for any aircraft, the XL configuration cuts the total drag of the load in two ways. Firstly, the big wing means that each bomb or missile can be carried individually, so that the big multiple ejector racks and long pylons of earlier aircraft can be eliminated. Secondly, for the same reason, the stores can be carried in tandem rows; a rule of thumb states that the second bomb in a row generates half the drag of the first, and that the third produces half the drag of the second.

Shades of the XL can also be seen in the British Aerospace ACA (Agile Combat Aircraft) which could form the basis for a European multinational fighter in the 1990s. The ACA carries weapons in a very similar fashion, and the main difference between the two configurations is that the ACA has a shorter-chord wing and a foreplane. This is known as 'semi-conformal' weapon carriage, and will probably be featured on the ATF. The B-1B uses the same technique to carry a heavy load of cruise missiles, while the Tornado and the McDonnell Douglas dual-role Eagle use tandem weapons carriage. The ATF, though, may go further, into the world of 'conformal' weapons. These could be special dispensers, tailored to the aircraft design and carrying guided submunitions. However, it is quite certain that, even in the late 1990s, the capability to haul standard iron bombs will be needed. Smart weapons may be individually effective, but no fighter commander will ever feel that he has enough of them.

Another traditional weapon to find a place on the ATF will be a gun. The development of aircraft guns has not been fast or revolutionary, and the weapon itself is likely to represent an incremental improvement over current guns. It will probably be a Gatling-type weapon, with individually loaded revolving barrels. Its calibre will be greater than that of the current 20 mm M61A1 Vulcan, and it will have a higher velocity; combined, the two will give it much greater single-shot lethality. What will make it a truly dangerous weapon, though, is the sort of flight control/fire control coupling described in Chapter 2.

ATF will probably be a big aircraft. Small aircraft, the US Air Force found, tended not to meet the range requirements without external fuel. However, bigger aircraft, such as the SR-71-like 50-tonner mooted by Lockheed, were so expensive that not all the Air Force's objectives could be covered within a realistic budget. Even so, the Air Force's happy medium has fallen in the same size class as the Grumman F-14 Tomcat, that is to say, slightly bigger than the F-15.

Left: The second strand of combat aircraft away from the super complex and super capable advanced technology fighter is the lightweight dogfighter with new technology packed into a small 'agile' airframe. BAe's private venture advanced combat aircraft will not feature swept forward wings as in this Ferranti concept. **Above:** —nor necessarily will BAe's proposal for next generation supersonic V/STOL combat aircraft. This 1980 concept packs in virtually every fashionable airframe configuration

It follows that not all the world's fighters will be ATFs, because most other nations will not be able to afford such a large and potent machine. Once ATF is established in service, the US Air Force may well be looking at a cheaper aircraft. Much of the technology used in ATF is directly applicable to such a type. Lighter fighters now under development, such as the Saab JAS39 Gripen and IAI Lavy, use full-time fly-by-wire systems, composite structures, semi-conformal weapon carriage and advanced cockpit displays. Advanced aerodynamics are evident on the F-16XL, the British Aerospace ACA and the Dassault ACX. Future versions of these aircraft, developed in the 1990s, may incorporate as many ATF features as economic sense allows.

One area in which smaller fighters could well lead the way, though, is in field performance. Military planners are now looking again at the range of threats facing airfields, and wondering whether ATF's 500-yard field length might be a lot to expect after a withering shower of submunitions. The logical next step is Stovl, short take-off, vertical landing, as successfully practised for a decade by operational British Aerospace (BAe) Harrier fighters.

Unlike more conventional aircraft such as the ATF or the ACA, the advanced supersonic Stovl aircraft has yet to find a place in firm military development plans. Stovl aircraft tend to be more expensive than conventional aircraft of the same flight performance, and the argument for adding performance or numbers in the air with the help of a little cheap concrete on the ground is persuasive.

In some ways, too, the very potential of Stovl aircraft has created resistance. Their ability to operate from small, slow ships is, in theory, a great boost for naval air power. But the world of naval aviation is divided into the US Navy, with its mighty fleet of supercarriers, and the rest of the world with a handful of ships per country. The rest-of-the-world market is too small and scattered to sponsor expensive development programmes; the US Navy is so terrified by the prospect of armchair admirals promoting Stovl as a substitute for the supercarrier that it finds it difficult to consider it as anything but a threat.

THE STOVL SOLUTION

Over the long term, interest in Stovl will rise, for a number of reasons. One is the steady development of counter-airfield weapons. Conventional doctrine has held that only high-yield nuclear weapons could disable a well-defend airfield with protected hangars and ground facilities, but this is no longer the case. The short-field capability planned for ATF is a tremendous step forward, but the advanced Stovl aircraft offers further advantages. While Harriers generally need a similar take-off distance to that proposed for ATF, about 1200 feet, they have a much lower take-off speed, which helps operations from uneven surfaces. A future supersonic Stovl would have the same take-off speed combined with faster acceleration, and could lift off in a shorter distance at maximum take-off weight. The Stovl aircraft lands with zero run, so the commander is assured of his ability to recover his force, even if his field has been attacked or repair work interrupted.

Meanwhile, many of the features which conventional wisdom has cited as disadvantages of the Stovl type have been specified for the ATF. The added complexity of vectored thrust is one example. The short-landing aircraft also needs landing guidance and control systems, to help a tired fighter pilot make a pinpoint touchdown from a normal approach; bringing a vertical-landing aircraft down on to a precise spot is relatively easy. Work on future Stovl designs is under way in both Britain and the United States. A supersonic Stovl aircraft could be in service by the mid-1990s, and some early discussions about possible transatlantic collaboration have taken place.

The first issue is the design of any Stovl aircraft is to provide vertical thrust. Literally dozens of ways of doing this have been proposed, and not a few of them have been tested in flight. They have ranged in complexity from the tail-sitter or VATOL (vertical attitude take-off and landing), which needs no extra mechanical systems for lift, and just a simple low-speed control system, to a six-engined fighter with four engines in swivelling pods on the wingtips and two more installed vertically in the fuselage. Most have failed, more or less abysmally. The mediocre Soviet Yak-36 has seen limited service, but because it is limited to vertical take-off it cannot lift more than 80 per cent or so of its installed thrust, and is therefore heavy and inefficient.

The only high-performance Stovl type to see service has been the BAe Harrier, of which nearly 300 have been built. Another 400 of the improved Harrier II, developed by McDonnell Douglas for the US Marine Corps and the RAF, are on order. The Harrier's design is based on the concept of vectored thrust, in which the exhaust stream is deflected 90 degrees by swivelling nozzles and cascade vanes. Its Pegasus engine is a turbofan, and is mounted well forward in the airframe; the fan and core exhaust separately, forward and aft of the centre of gravity, so that the thrust vector passes through the centre of gravity of the aircraft.

The success of the Harrier makes its layout very attractive as a basis for a future supersonic Stovl aircraft. In fact, the development of such a machine started nearly a quarter of a century ago, but was cancelled in 1964. Now, development work has started again. The fundamental change between the Harrier and the new aircraft is the addition of afterburners to the front nozzles, a technique called plenum-chamber burning (PCB). PCB provides added vertical thrust at the front of the engine, so that the thrust can still pass through the centre of gravity. It gives the engine the thrust/weight ratio and exhaust velocity for supersonic flight and transonic manoeuvre, and by improving the thrust/weight ratio it improves the overall performance of the aircraft.

PCB presents a number of technical challenges, and these are being addressed in current development work. One of the most basic problems is maintaining a stable and efficient burn in a very cool, low-velocity airstream; aerodynamically sophisticated swirling burners, designed using advanced computer simulations of the airflow, have to be fitted into the short space between the fan and the nozzle. The PCB systems on both sides of the engine must light reliably and simultaneously. Efficiency requires the use of variable nozzles, with their control or actuation mechanisms passing through the swivelling joint. Another problem area is common to many high-speed Stovl aircraft. Like any aircraft with reheat, they produce a huge volume of hot exhaust air. Conventional aircraft simply leave it behind, but a hovering jet could re-ingest the hot air into its engine intakes, causing the engine to overheat very quickly. (As with the ATF's supersonic-cruise powerplant, the temperature rise is multiplied by the engine pressure ratio.) A Harrier fitted with an augmented Pegasus has been suspended from a Victorian gantry crane to investigate the 'recirculation' effect.

BAe has completed a mock-up of a supersonic Stovl design, the P.1216, but has not revealed any details of the layout. It could take advantage of modern aerodynamic and flight-control technology, by using an aerodynamically unconventional configuration tailored to the needs of the propulsion system. A canard layout, for example, would allow the engine to be installed well forward in a reasonably efficient supersonic aircraft.

A supersonic Stovl would almost certainly need a completely new engine to replace the Pegasus. For one thing, advancing technology makes it possible to create a lighter and more efficient engine; for another, the Pegasus would probably not be adequate for a supersonic aircraft. A key issue is

the provision of low-to-zero-airspeed control. The supersonic aircraft will be no larger in dimensions than the Harrier, but will be heavier and more powerful. It will therefore need a much more powerful version of the Harrier's reaction control system (RCS), which directs high-pressure air from the engine through variable nozzles at the nose, tail and wingtips to control the aircraft at speeds where aerodynamic controls are useless. Bleeding such a large quantity of high-pressure air from the engine is no small consideration, because it robs the core of its working fluid at a critical point in the cycle, and can badly affect the efficiency of the engine.

The need for a more powerful RCS, though, could well be offset by improved control technology. NASA's Ames Research Centre is acquiring a Harrier airframe (one which had been modified to demonstrate Harrier II technology) and plans to fit it with a new, integrated flight and propulsion control system. One aim of the programme is to demonstrate reduced RCS loads; the idea is that a sensitive, automated control system can catch and correct deviations from the intended flightpath before they become serious, and can therefore make use of lower power. Another possibility is that small variations in the front and rear nozzle angles could be used to trim the aircraft in hovering flight, something which must currently be done by the RCS. The new control system is also designed to make the aircraft easier to fly, especially in difficult circumstances such as night or bad-weather ship landings.

While the Harrier's track record, coupled with the backing which the vectored-thrust concept enjoys from the USMC and RAF, puts the smart money on PCB for a future Stovl fighter, there are a number of other candidate technologies around. Some are more active than others. Lift-plus-lift/cruise combines a vectored-thrust main engine with auxiliary lift engines; it can be quite easily integrated into a conventional supersonic layout, but has fallen into disfavour because of its weight and complexity. RALS (remote augmented lift system) is somewhat similar, but instead of lift engines it uses a lighter, simpler augmentor fed with low-pressure air from the main engine's fan section.

One quite promising system, based on the use of ejectors or jet-pumps, has been developed by de Havilland Canada (DHC). An ejector is an open-ended duct into which a high-pressure, high-speed airstream is injected through a nozzle half-way along its length. A combination of friction, mixing effects and pressure differentials draws outside air into the duct, and creates a high-mass, low-velocity airstream which is very efficient at the low airspeeds encountered in the case of a hovering Stovl aircraft. The improved propulsive efficiency

Above left: Hinting perhaps more accurately at the actual shape of supersonic Stovl from British Aerospace in this wind tunnel model with a four poster vectored thrust layout.

Above right: SAAB's JAS 39 Gripen is another contender in the fly by wire, canard layout, artifically stable combat aircraft line up. While the pressure of research costs are pushing Britain, France and Germany's advanced fighter programmes together, Sweden and Israel are going it alone while Dassault's ACX (left) waits for suitors. The ACX, like the others, features full-time fly by wire, composite structures and conformal weapons carriage

The McDonnell Douglas Model 279-3 is a proposal for a shipboard V/STOL aircraft capable of supersonic flight powered by a Pegasus-type engine with plenum chamber burning

means that the ejector can boost the thrust available from a jet engine by as much as 70 per cent.

Ejectors have been fitted to experimental aircraft before, with a total lack of success. In the real world, augmentation ratios have never reached predicted levels. The DHC ejector, though, has been successful in rig tests. It is designed to be built into the wing of a delta-winged aircraft. The nozzles are built into the wing roots, along the side of the fuselage, and the walls of the duct are formed by the fuselage side and the ejector covering door. In this way, it is possible to build a large-volume duct into a small supersonic airframe.

General Dynamics has used the DHC ejector concept in the design of an experimental aircraft, the E7. It would be powered by a single turbofan engine, with the core flow passing through a 2-D augmented nozzle. The fan flow would feed a separate duct, feeding either the ejectors or an augmented forward-thrust nozzle.

Technical questions on the DHC ejector include the drag that it would develop in transition, which could be very high. Its advantages include the fact that it would not produce a destructively hot vertical exhaust, giving it a 'benign footprint' in Stovl jargon, and abundant take-off and landing thrust with moderate fuel consumption. A large-scale model of the E7 is to be built and tested in NASA's 40-foot × 80-foot wind tunnel at Ames.

Another new concept, at an earlier stage of development, is the 'tandem fan', considered very promising by Rolls-Royce. The starting point for the tandem fan is a conventional augmented turbofan engine, but the first two stages of the fan are separated from the last stage and the core engine by a long driveshaft and straight duct. This transfer section incorporates an arrangement of cascades, auxiliary inlets and blockers which can separate the engine airflow into two streams. Air entering the main inlet passes through the front fan stages and exhausts vertically through a separate outlet, directly behind the fan. The rear fan stage and core breathe through auxiliary inlets and exhaust at the rear, through an augmented nozzle. Rolls-Royce has designed a version of this system, called a hybrid fan, in which the front stream exhausts through vectorable nozzles.

SUPERSONIC STOVL

The tandem fan would take a great deal of development, but has a great deal of potential. It obtains increased thrust for vertical flight through increased mass flow, like the ejector, so it has a benign footprint, no recirculation problem and low fuel consumption on landing and take-off. Its vertical flight mode

Another solution in getting high performance aircraft to sea is 'Vatol', vertical attitude take off and landing, with which the US Navy briefly flirted in the early 1950s. This proposal might be more successful

could also be adapted to provide very efficient subsonic cruise power. The technical issues involved could mean that the tandem fan is best seen as a follow-on to a first-generation, PCB-powered supersonic Stovl.

Advanced supersonic Stovl aircraft will bring the benefits of Stovl to a wider variety of missions. By the year 2000, they could be replacing types like the F-16 and Harrier II for offensive support, moving quickly to suppress threatening artillery or missile systems, engaging enemy support aircraft and hitting armour with multiple-warhead munitions. They will operate with relative immunity from counter-air operations; advanced electronic systems, with their capacity for self-test and self-diagnosis and their ability to function after partial failures, will make the Stovl fighter reliable and rugged for off-base operation. The sort of technology that is applied to the ATF in search of ultimate performance against high-value targets will be adapted to another end in the Stovl fighter, to give it quick reaction and high reliability. It will be a tough, independent, 'kick the starter and jump aboard' fighting machine.

Undoubtedly, the supersonic Stovl will be developed in parallel for naval operations. The Harrier has already demonstrated that a Stovl aircraft designed purely for land-based operation needs no modification to operate from a ship. As the development of the Sea Harrier shows, however, the shipboard version of a future Stovl will have rather different equipment and weapons, suited to its likely targets; it will have a powerful radar, and developed, long-range versions of missiles such as the AIM-120 or the anti-ship Sea Eagle. It might well carry longer-range weapons such as Stealth cruise missiles.

Given the armoury of advanced weapons that it will need, and the sophistication of its systems, the naval Stovl will not be found on the helideck of the average frigate. Neither will it be routinely operated off a converted merchant ship. Tailored Stovl carriers will be real warships, well protected and well defended and with plenty of capacity for weapons; it will not make sense to put the Stovl fighter on anything less.

Stovls will find a place aboard conventional supercarriers as well, for a number of good reasons. They can be launched regardless of relative wind, and without taking up time on the catapult. Likewise, they can be recovered without blocking the landing deck. Thanks to their ability to 'stop, and then land', as Stovl aviators put it, they can also operate in conditions which would halt normal carrier operations. In the Falklands, Harriers were recovered safely when forward visibility was less than the length of the carrier.

While the naval Stovl fighter will have a specially built carrier as its regular base, there will certainly be merchant-ship-based auxiliary carriers, possibly operating a mix of navy and air force aircraft. Fitted with prefabricated hangars and decks, and carrying containerised control and defence systems, these ships will support amphibious operations and long-distance deployments. For most countries, navy fighter forces will become the permanent core of their rapid-deployment air power, augmented by air force squadrons in time of need.

Mainstream maritime airpower will continue to be based on the supercarrier, and the conventional naval aircraft. In the year 2000, the US Navy will have added more ships to its supercarrier fleet, but even the USS *Forrestal*, an old lady of 45, may still be in active service. The Soviet Union is expected to have begun deployment of its own big-deck carriers, carrying a mix of Stovl and conventional aircraft. On current plans, the USN will still be using many of the same basic aircraft types. The service discussed an equivalent to the ATF, the proposed VFMX fighter/strike type, in the course of 1981, but has now dropped it in favour of modernising the types now in service. The Grumman Tomcat fighter, for example, will appear in the late 1980s in a new F-14D version, with new engines, completely revised radar and cockpit displays and provision for new missiles, and it is expected to be twice as effective as the F-14A. A new attack aircraft is to be developed from either the A-6 or the F-18.

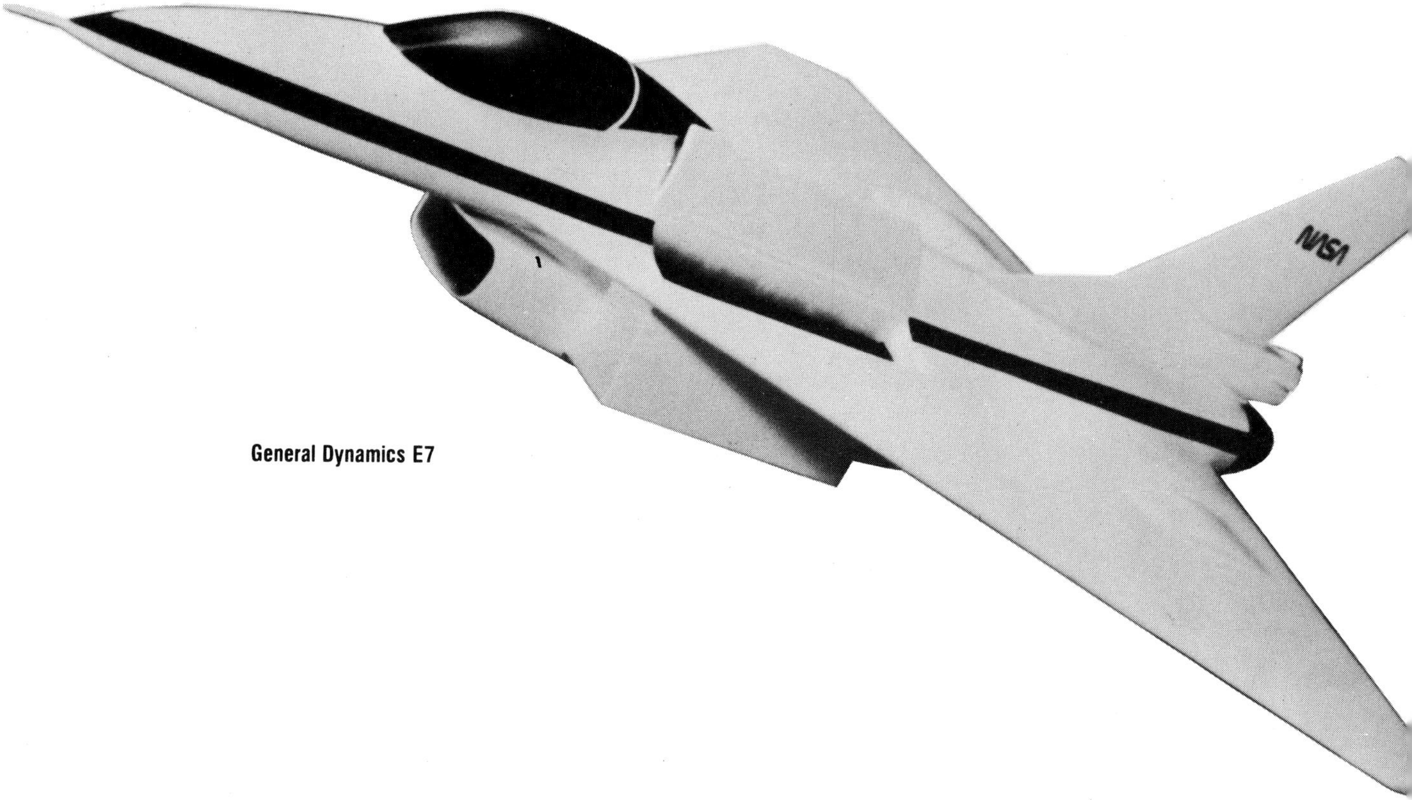

General Dynamics E7

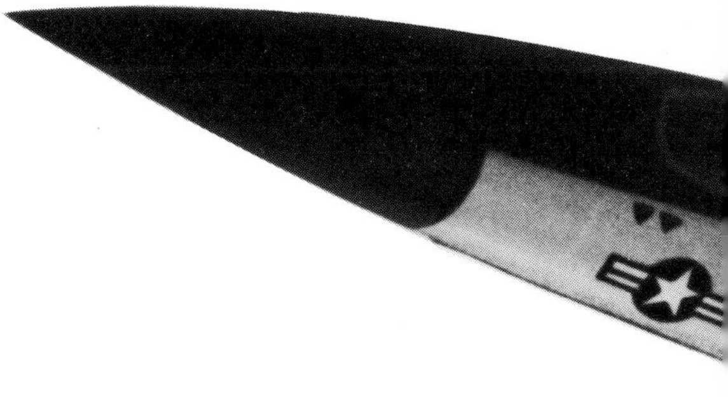

The F-18 Hornet seems set to continue US airpower at sea well into the next century. It will be joined by developments of the F-14 Tomcat in the fleet air defence role rather than a completely new aircraft

SUPERSONIC NAVAL V/STOL
US Navy sponsored studies of V/STOL configurations have covered a very wide range of concepts. Early work included lift plus lift-cruise proposals such as the General Dynamics GD 218. More recently the US Navy and NASA have looked at the promising tandem fan arrangement featured in the Vought TF-120 which has attracted some attention also from Rolls-Royce, and at an ejector concept developed by de Havilland Canada and incorporated in the General Dynamics E7 design

General Dynamics GD 218

Vought TF-120

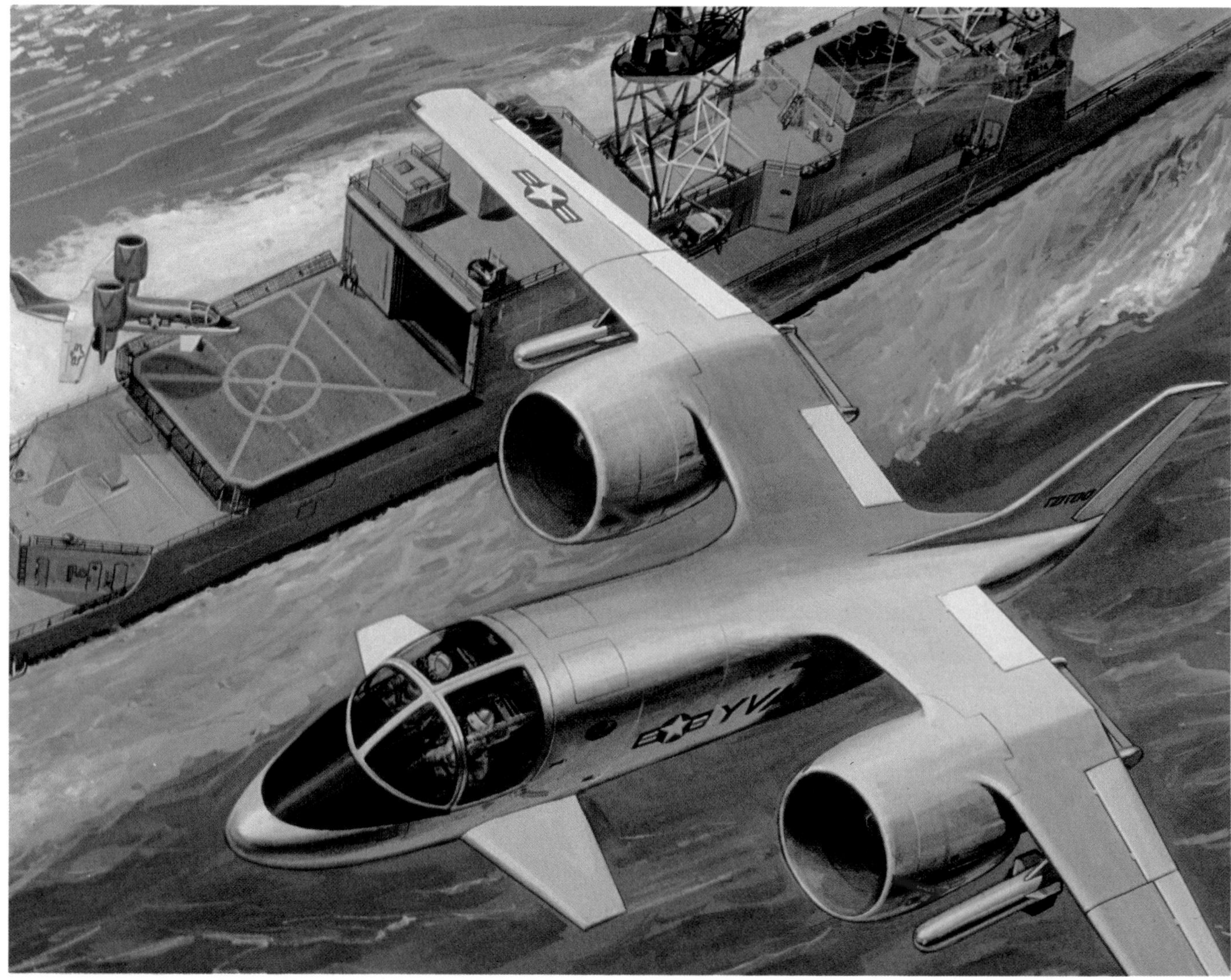

Development and definition of a wholly new naval aircraft is now unlikely to start in earnest before the end of the 1980s, and such a type would begin to enter service around the turn of the century. It might well, like ATF, be a dual-role fighter/attack aircraft, and would probably aim at highly supersonic performance and some Stealth characteristics. ATF-type Stovl techniques would make carrier operations easier, safer and more efficient.

Combat aircraft will, as always, take the bulk of the research and development money and most of the year-by-year procurement funds. Other military aircraft have tended to evolve more gradually, and will not have changed radically, at least in their external appearance, by the end of the century. In the case of some classes of aircraft the unchanged package will, paradoxically, be an indirect result of very important changes under the skin. These are the classes of aircraft which can be described as 'electronics-intensive' — flying platforms for sophisticated systems.

An excellent example of this class is the anti-submarine warfare (ASW) aircraft. In the year 2000, the US Navy (whose ASW fleet is at least equal to the rest of the world's total) will probably be using a development of today's Lockheed P-3 Orion. It may have new engines, a longer fuselage and an extended wing, but will still be instantly recognisable as a P-3, a 40-year old basic design. The P-3, and aircraft like it, will have survived because it makes more sense to spend money on new radar equipment, improved sonar systems and, above all, powerful computing and display systems than to pursue the marginal improvements possible with a new air-frame.

Another likely survivor, from the same company, is the U-2/TR-1 high-altitude surveillance platform. The aircraft exists, its development is paid for, and despite its age it is very difficult to improve on its altitude, payload and endurance. It is also designed so that new 'payloads' (surveillance or communications equipment) can be built into removable pallets and pods, and simply installed in the aircraft.

High-capacity communications links and long-range surveillance systems will create a need for communications and surveillance aircraft, the airborne watchtowers of the 'extended battlefield'. There is an active controversy in this area, typified in the current US programme to develop a long-range, high-resolution radar system to pinpoint tank formations behind enemy lines. Some believe that the system will be more effective and more versatile if the radar and its

operators are carried aboard a Boeing 707; others contend that such a system represents too easy and too valuable a target for MiG-31 long-range fighters, and would rather put the operators in earthbound shelters and the electronics in a stealthy TR-1 at 75 000 feet. The outcome of this argument could have implications not only for this particular programme (the J-Stars, or joint surveillance and target acquisition radar system) but also for future successors to today's airborne warning and control system (AWACS) aircraft.

Future AWACS types, whether shipboard or land-based, may well lose their characteristic rotodomes in favour of advanced synthetic aperture radars that use rapid electronic switching to mimic the mechanical scanning techniques of current radars. These radars do not even need separate radomes; instead, the small transmitting and receiving elements could be arrayed along the fuselage sides and wing leading edges: a so-called 'conformal' radar, offering some of the performance advantages of a radar dish as big as the carrier aircraft's wingspan.

ADVANCED AIRLIFTERS

The USAF's new freighter for the 1990s, the McDonnell Douglas C-17, will be the most advanced aircraft of its type in the world. It will not incorporate any major technical advances, because its production has been deferred for several years to avoid a clash with B-1 and fighter production peaks; the design itself was defined in 1981.

One type which might emerge by the end of the 1990s is a replacement for the West's universal military transport, the Lockheed C-130 Hercules. A team of manufacturers, including Lockheed and many Airbus consortium members, agreed in 1983 to study such an aircraft, described as the Fima (future international multirole airlifter); Boeing also has a group keeping a close eye on the market.

Far left: One of the advantages of the CTOL (Conventional Take off and Landing) carrier is the ability to operate larger special purpose types such as early warning or ASW aircraft. This VTOL multi mission proposal from Vought would give much simpler ships the same capabilities

Above: A likely survivor of the year 2000 will be the US Navy's P-3 Orion anti submarine aircraft which has already gone through several comprehensive electronic updates since its operational debut in the early '60s

Right: The Sikorsky Sea Hawk, the US Navy's LAMPS III (Light Airborne Multipurpose System) helicopter which effectively acts as a computerised flying component of the ship in the ASW role is another system which is highly likely to be still be in service if not production inside the next century

Any design team looking at a C-130 replacement for the late 1990s has a wide range of operational needs to consider, and an equally varied assortment of potential technical solutions. A tactical airlifter, for example, should be capable of repeated operations from a quickly prepared airstrip. But how quickly should the airstrip be prepared? The amount of effort needed to accommodate and service different types of aircraft varies enormously. Army manpower is measured in battalion/days; a base for a Stol aircraft such as a de Havilland Buffalo can be prepared in 0·5 battalion/days, a C-130 base takes more than six times as much effort, and a base for heavy airlifters such as C-5s and C-141s takes 60 battalion/days to build. The length of runway is not the only factor concerned; 'flotation', or the load imposed on the runways and taxiways, is also important. Good flotation is desirable, but costly, demanding a heavy and bulky landing gear.

The load which an airlifter needs to carry is a source of unlimited debate and discussion, and is as fundamental to the design as the runway requirement. Military loads include extremely dense objects, such as armoured vehicles, and very large, relatively light objects such as helicopters. Even a C-5, for example, cannot carry an intact Chinook; disassembled for air transport, the Chinook takes three days and a flight test to be put back in flying condition. The C-17 is designed to carry a range of loads at least comparable to those of the much bigger C-5, and a future airlifter might continue this trend, accommodating similarly awkward loads within an even smaller gross weight.

Survivability will be another very important design issue. Unlike the larger freighters, the tactical airlifter cannot be confined to well secured bases. It must traverse disputed ground, even if it does not have to penetrate into the thick of active engagements. All in all, the advanced tactical airlifter will present an interesting design challenge, calling on much of the advanced technology which will be available by the 1990s.

Upper-surface-blowing (USB) configurations, although rejected by the USAF in favour of the C-17, promise not only excellent Stol performance but also improved low-speed climb and manoeuvre. For a combat airlifter this could be important, not only reducing the time during which it is most vulnerable to small SAMs, but also shrinking the perimeter within which they can be effectively fired and making it easier to secure a forward base.

An oversized cabin and landing gear are penalties which the tactical airlifter can tolerate; it is designed for utility rather than efficiency. Some Boeing studies, envisaging an aircraft which could carry a light, bulky load such as a Chinook over long distances, have questioned the need for pressurisation in the hold of a specialised aircraft, and this would considerably reduce the weight penalty of a large cabin.

Survivability can be approached in a number of ways. USB offers natural infra-red shielding for the exhaust, but requires big-fan engines which tend to have high radar visibility from the front. An extended inlet with a radar-absorbent, movable plug might alleviate the problem at some cost in weight and

The McDonnell Douglas C-17 is planned to give power projection forces the ability to fly over long ranges yet make landings at the heart of the contended area offloading troops straight into action

Backbone of the USAF's current strategic airlift capability is the fleet of giant Lockheed C-5 Galaxies, progressively being reworked to C-5B standard with new wings

Above: The McDonnell Douglas KC-10 Extender tanker transport began to enter USAF service in the early 1980s after several funding cutbacks. It provides a significant increase in the US's strategic lift plus deployment flexibility for strategic and tactical aircraft, the key to true superpower intervention capability

Above right: The legendary Herk will be still be in very widespread service in the year 2000 although a replacement would be a huge industrial prize. **Right:** Stalwarts of US airlift, the C-141B Starlifter and the C-130 Hercules. A replacement aircraft might ideally combine the one's long distance performance with the other's tactical short field capability, plus low-level, all weather operability and electronic countermeasures to ensure its survival

efficiency, and key areas such as the wing and empennage leading edges could also be treated with radar-absorbent materials. Highly automated active and passive counter-measure systems would be standard. The most important survival feature, however, might be the ability to fly at low level in any weather, using passive infra-red systems and hard-to-detect scanning lasers for terrain avoidance.

COMBAT AIRLIFTERS

A large aircraft such as a combat airlifter also offers considerable scope for design features which allow it to take hits and not only survive, but also complete its mission. 'Adaptive' fly-by-wire systems, combined with multiple control surfaces, could assess the effects of battle damage and reconfigure the aircraft to fly as efficiently as possible within seconds of a hit, and without any intervention by the pilot. Electronic and optical control systems can be much more easily protected and more easily distributed around the aircraft than mechanical control runs, and are less likely to be hit in the first place. The same comparison would apply to all-electric actuation of control surfaces, which would be vastly less vulnerable than a hydraulic system. For critical areas such as the cockpit and the engines, advanced composites can provide a great deal of

U.S. ARMY

The Hughes AH-64A Apache, the US Army's hugely complex (and expensive) tank killer. The nose turret mounted Target Acquisition and Designation System provides laser designation for the Apache's Hellfire missiles while the Pilot's Night Vision System ensures the Apache can operate in darkness, in bad weather and in the fog of battle armour protection at a relatively modest cost in weight.

The final issue is whether it will be possible to provide such an aircraft at a reasonable cost, or whether the market for an aircraft that can do so is large enough to justify the expense of development. Many operators, after all, use the C-130 as a general-purpose transport; Fima could accordingly emerge as a design biased more towards efficient long-distance haulage than towards Stol and combat. The advanced airlifter will probably not appear until the later 1990s, at best, if only because the major customer, the USAF, will not start its definition until the C-17 is well established in production.

For big changes in military aircraft technology in the next few years, other than the first-line fighters and bombers, it is necessary to look outside the world's air forces, to the only class which is most widely used by another armed service — the helicopter. What may be the most significant development in the history of the military rotocraft is emerging from a long and intense process of debate and analysis within the US Army, concerning the nature of the air-land battle, the war of ground troops and systems, and their air and missile support resources, around the turn of the century. The outcome of the tacticians' deliberations, discussions and computer models was the sometimes controversial Airland 2000 concept, revealed in 1981.

Airland 2000 is a highly complex subject, and there is no space here to treat it fully. From the viewpoint of military aviation, however, the most important aspect of Airland 2000 is that it envisages the end of a clear, defined picture of front lines and columns. Instead, the Airland 2000 battlefield will be extended through the use of highly accurate stand-off weapons of various types. As the fighting is drawn out over a wider area, active engagements will form 'islands of conflict' throughout the battlefield.

While the islands themselves will be packed with firepower, the rest of the battlefield will be hostile enough to prevent

Below: Westland's Lynx 3 proposal, seen here in wooden mock up, is optimised for anti tank warfare with a mast mounted sight and laser designator in the nose

Right: Bell's Acap (Advanced Composite Airframe Programme) demonstrator makes extensive use of composite materials in the airframe and rotor and is a component of the US Army's huge LHX programme

normal surface movement. Neither will the islands present any well defined landing zones. Airland 2000 implies a high degree of dependence on the helicopter for supply, communications and control, despite the fact that the entire battlefield area will contain threats to the helicopter's own survival; the most important of these could be the enemy helicopter.

The first and most important helicopter programme to emerge since Airland 2000 was formulated is LHX (light helicopter-experimental). If LHX does all that it is supposed to, it will mark an immense step forward in the military use of the helicopter, to the point where the helicopter will equal the tank in importance as a land warfare system.

Light military helicopters have previously been designed as light transport vehicles, flying Jeeps, in a sense, and adapted to various missions with bolt-on equipment such as missile pylons, gun pods and sighting systems. LHX, by contrast, is designed as a combat aircraft. The primary objective is to design a vehicle that can survive through self-defence, the use of terrain and weather for concealment, and reduced observables. Higher cost and a more modest payload are being accepted for LHX, on the simple grounds that a traditional light helicopter will not stand a chance of survival in the Airland 2000 battle.

Bottom left: The Franco-German PAH-2 mock up designed primarily as an anti tank machine rather than a helicopter 'dogfighter'

Bottom right: Before the full LHX programme is implemented, the US Army's AHIP (advanced helicopter improvement programme) will retrofit scout helicopters such as this Kiowa with mast mounted sights and new weapon systems

BATTLEFIELD HELICOPTERS

The shape of LHX will depend entirely on the results of a study programme now under way, because this will determine how fast the aircraft needs to be. There is a trade-off between speed and manoeuvrability; the slower helicopter can hug the terrain more closely, because it takes less energy to follow a ground profile at a lower speed, and because the pilot has more time to observe the ground and take cover effectively. If the best speed for LHX turns out to be 300 mph or more, the only suitable configuration in sight is the Tilt-Rotor; at 250

Above: Boeing's LHX proposal features mast mounted target designation and no tail rotor

Left: Bell's XV-15 tilt rotor technology demonstrator led to the JVX military tilt-rotor programme. The US Air Force is interested in the type for special operations and the US Marine Corps for amphibious assault. This is Bell's concept for a militarised utility tilt-rotor

Right: Hughes Helicopters has made this distinctive LHX proposal for something very akin to a rotary wing fighter with notar and low drag hingeless rotor. The stub wings might carry anti-tank weapons or air to air weapons for combating enemy helicopters

mph, a compound helicopter with an auxiliary propulsion system would be adequate, and at 200 mph the requirement could be met by an advanced conventional helicopter. At the time of writing, the last seems most likely. The Tilt-Rotor is a complex aircraft, and excels in payload/range performance rather than manoeuvrability. Sikorsky has proposed an aircraft using its advancing blade concept (ABC) rotor combined with a ducted propulsor for horizontal thrust. It is a promising solution in many ways, but advances in conventional rotor technology have closed the gap between ABC and the standard helicopter in performance, while widening the difference in cost.

The advanced conventional helicopter will incorporate two important advances in its rotor system. It will use new blade aerofoils, with improved characteristics both at the high airspeeds attained by the advancing blade and the very low speeds at which the retreating blade operates, and it will have no pivots or hinges in its hub; instead, the rotors will be linked by composite beam structures, tailored to provide the right degree of damping in the flapping and lagging planes while offering minimum resistance in torsion. An integrated technology rotor (ITR) incorporating these features is to be tested in 1987 under NASA/US Army sponsorship. Advantages of the ITR include increased efficiency, particularly at high speed, and lower drag, a reduction in the number of parts, and lower maintenance costs. It is also expected to improve manoeuvrability, particularly in negative-g (downthrust).

The application of stealth technology to LHX is highly classified, as are most programmes of the sort. It is likely to be a rather different job from the development of a stealth fighter or bomber, because the helicopter designer is concerned with a slightly different set of observables. Radar, for example, is of relatively little use in detecting a helicopter, which usually operates at such low altitudes that it is masked by terrain, so reduced radar cross-section will probably not be allowed to affect the design to any great degree. Infra-red, by contrast, is much more important, because the helicopter generally engages its targets at short ranges, where infra-red radiation is less affected by the atmosphere; LHX will have very well-shielded engines. Noise reduction is also important for the helicopter, for the same reasons, and may lead to the elimination of the tail rotor from LHX in favour of the Hughes-developed Notar (no tail rotor) concept. Finally, the optical spectrum will not be overlooked, and LHX will be designed to be as small as possible from all aspects.

LHX will have a composite airframe, for the sake of efficiency, survivability and smoothness. Again, this technology is being developed through a flight demonstration programme; Bell and Sikorsky are working on composite-bodied helicopters under US Army contract. Flight controls will be electronic, or possibly optical, largely because such systems are easier to protect against small-arms fire than mechanical control runs.

Where LHX is planned to break entirely new ground, though, is in its weapon-aiming, flight-control and cockpit display subsystems. If possible, it is to be operated by a single pilot, saving the 600 lb total weight of a second crew member and the associated armour protection, cabin space and systems. To make this possible, LHX will be fitted with radar, low-light tv and forward-looking infra-red (FLIR) sensors, all coupled to a system which will actually recognise targets from an electronic library of distinctive electromagnetic, visual and thermal signatures. The system will also decide which of the targets has the highest priority, and slew the aircraft's narrow-angle weapon-aiming systems on to the target.

ADVANCED ROTORCRAFT

Threat-warning and countermeasures systems will also be automated, and the flight-control system will provide for automatic performance of certain manoeuvres. For example, the LHX pilot will be able to hover behind terrain cover and initiate an automatic pop-up manoeuvre. As the aircraft breaks cover, any targets in sight will be identified and the most dangerous will be designated, while infra-red or electronic countermeasures are automatically used against any close-in threats. The pilot has both hands free to select weapons and fire, before the flight control system, coupled to an inertial reference system, automatically returns the aircraft to its original position. New cockpit displays, such as wide-angle head-up displays on which FLIR images and symbology can be projected, will allow the pilot to absorb all this information.

The current Advanced Rotorcraft Technology Integration (ARTI) programme is largely aimed at cockpit design for LHX. Because of the great importance of systems to the LHX programme, manufacturers of electronics and airframes have teamed up early. In another very significant development late in 1983, McDonnell Douglas, which is not only the world's largest manufacturer of fighters but also a world leader in fighter cockpit design, acquired Hughes Helicopters, which builds the US Army's Apache heavy attack helicopter.

The development cost of the sophisticated LHX design will

be offset by building some 5000 aircraft in two versions: a single-seat scout aircraft and a light utility version, capable of lifting the US Army's Hummer multipurpose vehicle. Both will carry air-to-air missiles for self-defence against hostile helicopters. Although the US Army does not yet envisage using LHX as a primary means of defeating hostile helicopters, it will undoubtedly encounter helicopter opposition in the course of its design missions, which include escorting transport helicopters and spotting targets for heavy attack helicopters such as the AH-64.

LHX is the key to logistics in the Airland 2000 battle. The 'islands of conflict' will be cut off from supply by unprotected land vehicles, and armoured supply columns would be slow and costly. As yet, no plans exist for a fixed-wing transport which can use ultra-short strips and survive in the battle zone. Instead, transport helicopters will be used, escorted by flights of LHX which will observe, flush out and suppress hostile fire en route and at the destination.

These transport helicopters will probably be no larger than current types. Increased size in helicopters tends to imply higher observability, less manoeuvrability and greater vulnerability, along with increased payload value. Instead, the US Army is trying to reduce the volume of its logistics needs, scaling down equipment of all kinds. The primary transport helicopter in the year 2000 will almost certainly be an updated version of the Sikorsky Blackhawk with a low-drag, hingeless rotor.

Some of the trends in the design of larger helicopters are covered in Chapter 6; technology in Boeing Vertol's new Model 360 helicopter is directly applicable to the US Army's emerging requirement for a Chinook replacement. New transport helicopters will, like LHX, be able to cruise at speeds of 200 mph, more than 50 per cent faster than the normal cruising speed of current large helicopters. They will use similar rotor technology to the LHX, and similar advanced control and flight guidance systems; some of this technology will also be built into future versions of the Blackhawk and Apache. Flying at 200 mph and tree-top altitude, and prepared to counter any hostile fire within seconds, the helicopter supply formation of the year 2000 could be a difficult target.

The US joint-service Tilt-Rotor programme, JVX, is designed for different missions from the similarly sized Army transport helicopter. The Army, for example, plans to use it as a carrier for electronic equipment. The Marine Corps' interest in JVX stems from the fact that it allows the Corps' ships to launch an airborne assault from a safe stand-off position, outside missile range. The Navy and Air Force are both interested in the type for combat rescue, and the Air Force has an additional requirement for 'special operations' — long-range, covert infiltration of intelligence and sabotage teams.

The Tilt-Rotor is the most successful medium-speed V/Stol aircraft developed so far. It does not have quite the same vertical-lift capability as a helicopter, and is not as efficient as a fixed-wing aircraft in forward flight, but it comes close enough to substitute for either in many missions, and becomes steadily more capable than a helicopter as the mission range exceeds 200 nautical miles. In vertical flight, the Tilt-Rotor presents no more control problems than a helicopter; like a helicopter, but unlike a jet-lift V/Stol aircraft, the Tilt-Rotor has enormous reserves of inertia in its rotor system which can be tapped for rapid and accurate control response. Neither is it accompanied by the high-energy downwash blast which rules many V/Stol concepts out of the combat-rescue mission. The complex mechanical control system of the Bell XV-15 technology demonstrator will be replaced by fly-by-wire on the production aircraft, which will also feature an ingenious swivelling-wing concept to minimise demands on hangarage.

The success of the Tilt-Rotor demonstration has probably eliminated the chances of rival concepts such as the Grumman tilting-fan aircraft. However, JVX itself remains controversial. While the four services currently involved need about 1000 aircraft between them, the three with the biggest research and development resources, the Army, Navy and Air Force, do not regard JVX as a priority programme. However, the success of the Marine Corps in developing the AV-8B Harrier II, despite Navy indifference, is a good sign for the future of this currently controversial project.

As always, the development of military aircraft will continue to be the biggest single slice of the aerospace business. As the incorporation of stealth technology, Stovl, supercruise and advanced avionics begins in earnest, and aircraft which integrate one or more of these technologies appear in service, the scene will be more interesting than ever.

Above: Bell's XV-15 tilt rotor has shown itself in extensive tests to come pretty close to maximum efficiency in forward and vertical flight and at ranges beyond 250 km

Above: Boeing Vertol's Model 360 is proposed as a medium lift helicopter for the US Army and makes extensive use of composites in its airframe and rotors

The Sikorsky XH-59A ABC (Advancing Blade Concept) demonstrator uses two very stiff counter rotating coaxial rotors with two turbojets for forward thrust

0.5

Missiles
–Beyond the Manned Aircraft

US Patriot advanced surface to air missile

In the year 2000, guided missiles will have been operational for just over 50 years, but less than 20 years, say, one and a half generations of development, will have passed since precision-guided weapons first played a major and potentially decisive role in an actual conflict.

Disappointment has been a way of life for missile users. Not one of the guided missiles that the USAF and USN first took to Vietnam worked properly. Soviet surface-to-air missiles proved effective at first, if fired in huge and costly barrages, but put up a very weak show in the Lebanon in 1982. Much of the development work that goes into new missiles over the next few years will be devoted to ensuring that future missiles perform as advertised.

The key to this, and the most important single development in the field of missile technology, is the vast increase in the amount of computer power available within given boundaries of weight, electrical power requirements and cost. The impact of this new technology on missile development transcends any mere statistical comparison of computer-chip power. It goes to the heart of the central problem in missile design, which is to make the weapon ape the responses of a controlling intelligence.

As the importance of this central problem is being recognised, so the connection between two formerly separate categories of military vehicle, missiles and remotely piloted vehicles (RPVs), has been realised. Grouped together as unmanned vehicle systems (UVS), they are now seen as presenting many common challenges. The boundaries between missiles and other UVSs are blurred, and many developments in missile technology are equally applicable to other types of UVS.

Any UVS involves many technologies, just like a manned aircraft; important development areas include propulsion, the airframe, sensors and warhead. Unlike a manned aircraft, though, the UVS requires some form of superior control before these technologies can be assembled into an operational system. Also, simply improving a UVS in one area may have only a marginal effect on its capability if the control system cannot be improved to exploit the improvement; for instance, a motor improvement may double a missile's range, but the miss distance may double too if the accuracy is not improved. On the other hand, an improvement in the control system can radically enhance the effectiveness of the entire missile, as in the case of the AIM-9L Sidewinder or BAe Sky Flash, both of which represent a great advance over the earlier Sidewinder and the Sparrow, from which they were developed. This will continue to hold true over the next decade, with the result that the external shape of the missile may change relatively little.

AUTONOMOUS MISSILES

There are three primary qualities that will be sought in the new generation of missiles. Two of them, reliability and probability of kill (PK) have been established for many years as

The MX intercontinental ballistic missile is fired from a test stand. The MX, now named 'Peacekeeper' may be deployed in one hundred ex-Minuteman silos in the American mid-west by the 1990s although it is still not politically in the clear

the main parameters of missile effectiveness. The third is now becoming more important, and will benefit more than most from new electronic technology. It is 'autonomy', sometimes called 'fire and forget', or the missile's independence from outside guidance sources. Autonomy renders the missile immune from the jamming of communications links, and frees the launcher to engage another target or take evasive action. Applied to a non-missile UVS, autonomy reduces the load on the data link, often the most difficult part of the design.

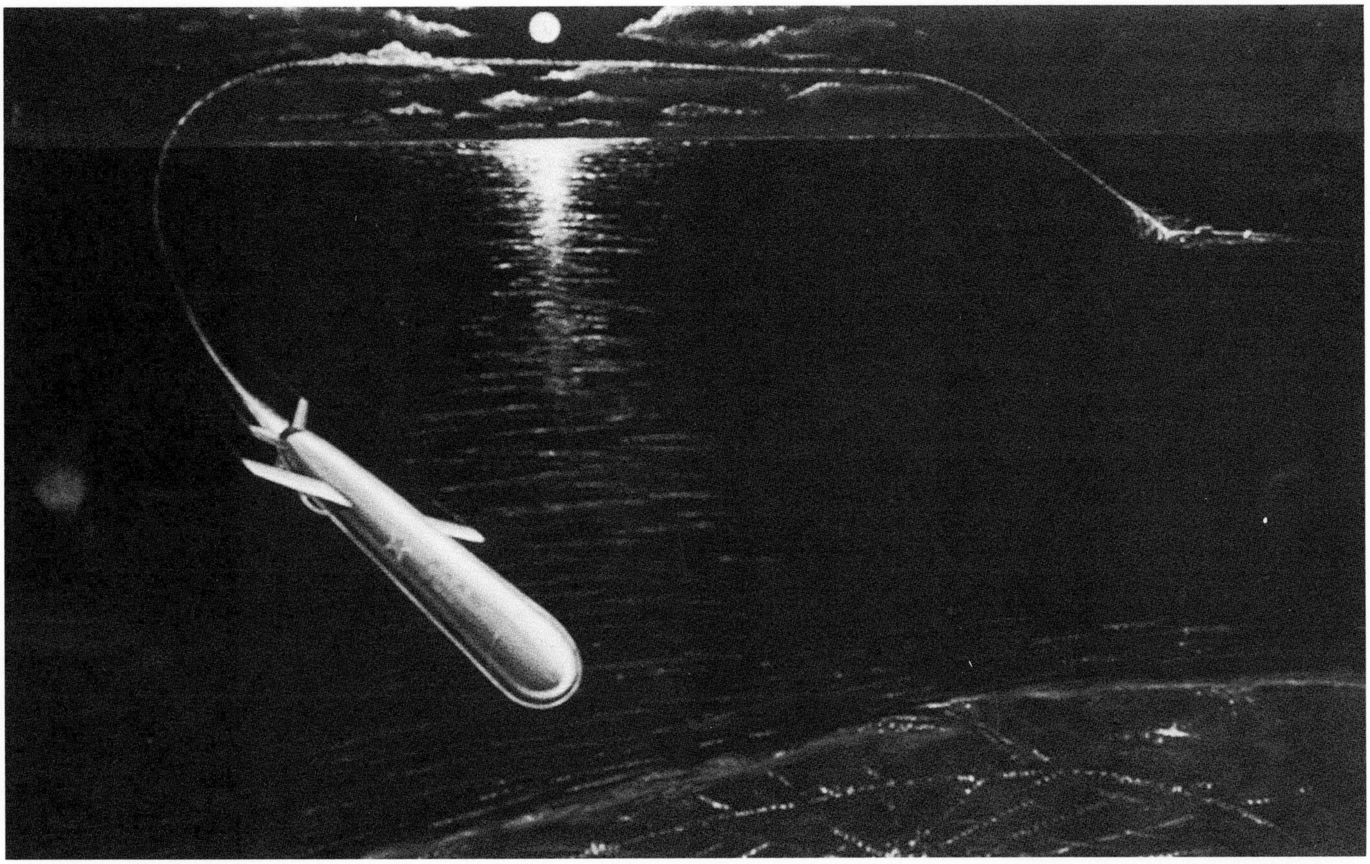

Some missiles have always been autonomous; these include the largest of all weapons, the intercontinental ballistic missile (ICBM), which has now been refined to the point where its frightening destructive power is matched by remarkable accuracy. Indeed, the part of an ICBM system which attracts the greatest attention is not the missile itself, but the way in which it is protected from destruction before launch: its 'basing mode', in nuclear jargon.

Basing mode has been the main issue in the argument over the new MX ICBM, and in the decision to limit its production in favour of a small ICBM (SICBM). Originally, the MX was to have been made mobile, but the logistic problems involved in moving such a vast weapon led to the demise of the plan. The SICBM, carrying only one warhead, will be far smaller and easier to move.

The USAF seems anxious to avoid repeating the long argument over basing mode that affected the MX programme, in which every conceivable means of launching the missile, from giant aircraft to small submarines, was studied and rejected. SICBM basing studies seem to centre on versions of a tortoise-like vehicle, carrying a single missile beneath an armoured, electromagnetically protected carapace. On warning of an attack, the tortoise would stop and lower its carapace, and air pumps would suck it down to the road. In this way, the missile could be protected from quite severe overpressures.

The US Department of Defense released this impression of a Soviet SS-NX-21 sea launched cruise missile in 1984. US forces deploy cruise missiles in air, ground and sea launched forms with advanced technology replacements under development

Development of the SICBM, and the appearance of potentially mobile ICBMs in the Soviet Union, indicate that neither superpower is ready to commit itself entirely to the sea-launched ballistic missile (SLBM). The SLBM seems to suffer from an incurable limit to accuracy, because the launch point cannot be determined with as much precision and consistency as that of a land-based weapon. On the other hand, development of a key component needed for the SICBM, a smaller, lighter guidance system offering the same accuracy as the MX system, will lead across to improved SLBMs.

ICBM development will be strongly affected, though, by the success or otherwise of current efforts to develop and define a space-based defensive system against ballistic missiles (see Chapter 3). The development of alternative strategic missiles will be pursued as a back-up, and to support the continued use of a full 'triad' of offensive systems.

The most important of these will be vastly improved cruise missiles, extremely difficult to intercept and capable of

BEFORE FLIGHT

Cruise missiles in their land, sea and here air launched varieties greatly multiply the number of platforms that can carry strategic weapons although they depend on satellite mapping for their accuracy

Vought's Improved Lance surface to surface missile could deliver swarms of 'smart' submunitions over armour concentrations with all the stopping power of a tactical nuclear weapon

operating over very long ranges. The cruise is a fundamentally different system from the ICBM. Its accuracy is not critically dependent on a precisely fixed launch point; it delivers its warhead more efficiently, and is therefore far smaller and lighter than the ballistic weapon, and this in turn makes it cheaper. Current cruise missiles are limited in range and accuracy, but future weapons of this type will be very different.

The current cruise missile was developed and fielded quite rapidly, using much off-the-shelf technology. Its construction drew on traditional missile techniques, and its engine and fuel were derived from manned-aircraft types. Immense improvements are possible by incorporating more advanced technology, particularly technology developed purely for the cruise missile.

STEALTH CRUISE

Two developments in this area are already well under way: the General Dynamics ACM (advanced cruise missile) and the Lockheed/US Navy stealth cruise missile. ACM will replace the current AGM-86B air-launched cruise missile in the late 1980s and early 1990s; the Lockheed/USN weapon is probably on the point of entering service, if it has not already done so, and is intended for use against heavily defended Soviet ships. Both weapons take full advantage of stealth technology. The cruise missile is almost the perfect application for stealth configurations; at some small penalty in lift/drag ratio, it might be possible to create a wingless, flattened shape with a minuscule radar cross-section. The new missiles presumably use passive guidance systems, radar-absorbent materials and engine shielding.

The next step in cruise missiles, though, is the incorporation of new propulsion and guidance technology. Cruise missile propulsion systems differ fundamentally from those of a manned aircraft in that their life cycles are measured in hours, not thousands of hours, so that engine life and the cost of fuel are almost irrelevant to the life-cycle cost of the system. The cruise missiles of the mid-1990s will burn exotic fuels such as slurries of high-energy materials, carbon or boron, for instance, suspended in specially formulated hydrocarbon bases. These fuels have far higher energy concentrations per unit of weight than even the special fuels used by current cruise missiles, allowing the missile to fly further on the same fuel load. They are also denser that current fuels, so the same weight occupies less volume and the size, and therefore the drag, of the entire vehicle can be reduced.

The engine of the advanced cruise missile may well be the first to make extensive use of ceramics in the combustor and the turbine section. Ceramics insulate instead of conducting, and thus reduce the losses incurred by cooling metal components in a normal engine. The other new feature of the advanced cruise engine could be a 'recuperative' or regenerative cycle, in which the wasted heat energy in the exhaust is fed back into the engine by a heat exchanger or recuperator. The engine can then attain its design pressure and temperature ratios using up to 25 per cent less fuel, and the recuperation system also reduces the infra-red signature of the engine. The problem which has frustrated the use of recuperators in aircraft has been the impossibility of developing a reasonably

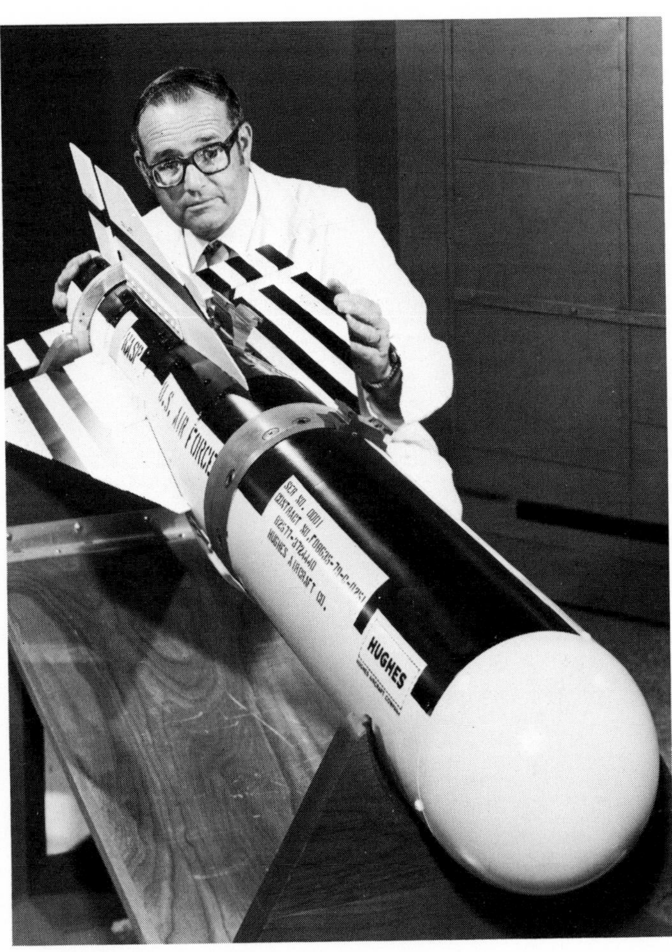

The Hughes WASP anti armour missile is designed for completely autonomous operations against armour. Launched by aircraft at stand off range, a salvo of wasps would automatically home on their targets using their own infra red or millimetric radar guidance

sized, long-lasting recuperator, but the difficulty may be eased with a short-life engine.

EXTENDING THE RANGE

The combined effect of radical engine cycles and exotic fuels is immense. The US Defense Advanced Research Projects Agency is now studying a cruise missile, no larger than the current weapons, with a true intercontinental range of nearly 8000 miles. Its systems would take advantage of the miniaturisation and power increases possible with VHSIC electronic technology. Its primary guidance system would be inertial, but it would home on its targets using passive optical systems, or scanning lasers, combined with a target recognition system which would compare the sensor images to a vast library of targets. This 'autonomous terminal homing' system would be so accurate that the weapon would be lethal against many targets even if armed with a non-nuclear warhead. The 'supercruise' would also be equipped to detect defensive systems, and alter course to avoid them while continuing to make progress towards its target. In many ways, it would be much harder to stop than an ICBM; although it would be much slower, its path is unpredictable, it would be a tiny target, its launch would be undetectable and it could take advantage of terrain masking.

Target recognition is a highly important technology for a wide range of systems, turning the simple sensor such as radar or forward-looking infra-red (FLIR) into a semi-intelligent observer. Current systems are developing some degree of intelligence, BAe's Sea Eagle missile, for instance, can be programmed before launch to attack only ships above a certain size, and higher computer power will make it possible to store images of targets in the weapon's memory and compare them to the sensor image within a tiny fraction of a second. These images will be three-dimensional, so that the target can be recognised from any angle, and multi-spectral; infra-red, visual and electromagnetic signatures will be compared to discriminate between, say, a live tank, a wrecked and abandoned tank and a decoy. While aircraft-borne systems will be the first to demonstrate genuine target recognition, missiles will follow close behind.

Cruise missiles of one kind and another will continue to grow in importance. They are flexible, in that a single airframe design can be used for a number of different missions. Because they are quite efficient at carrying military loads, they tend to be small in comparison to their range and yield, and this has benefits in all directions, smaller weapons are harder to detect, are cheaper to build and need fewer or cheaper launch platforms.

An example of many of these trends is the Northrop NV-150, proposed to the USAF in 1983. Designed for use against 'second echelon' armoured forces, the NV-150 has a plastic, reduced-observables airframe, a simple turbofan engine and a laser-gyro inertial navigation system, updated by navigational-satellite data, which contains no moving parts. All the main components are designed for low cost, and the missile would cost some $300 000 per round.

The NV-150 illustrates another very important trend, the development of tactical missiles into carrier vehicles for multiple small weapons, known collectively as submunitions. Underlying this change is the power of modern-technology non-nuclear warheads. The use of chemical explosives has now reached the point where the only surface targets which merit the use of a heavy single warhead are ships and fortifications. Take, for example, the SG357 anti-runway munition developed as part of the British JP233 airfield-attack weapon. About the size of a waste-paper basket, the SG357 contains three charges, which detonate in sequence. The first is a hollow charge which punches a hole into the runway. The second charge thrusts the weapon into the hole, where the third charge explodes; the trapped explosion breaks the concrete and heaves it upwards. The damage is far harder to repair than the crater caused by the heaviest conventional bomb, because the massive broken slabs must be lifted before the crater can be filled.

Unguided submunitions have been developed for use against area targets such as airfields and surface-to-air missile sites; the next stage is the development of precision-guided submunitions (PGSM) for use against small, mobile, protected targets such as tanks. One of the most extraordinary weapons in this category is the Avco Skeet. A small, saucepan-shaped object with a short wing in place of the handle, the Skeet is

spun into the air and flies a wobbly path over a tank formation, its infra-red detector scanning the ground as the vehicle oscillates. When the detector signals the presence of a tank, the Skeet detonates above it; an explosive charge instantly forges the weapon's heavy metal base into a hypersonic slug, which hits the tank with enough force to pierce its top armour and destroy it. Skeets can be scattered from an airborne dispenser, but the alternative launcher is even more remarkable. A device resembling a small interplanetary lander is dispensed from a container and descends by parachute. Acoustic sensors detect the approach of a vehicle, measure its range and bearing and determine whether it is a tank. If a tank comes within range, the launcher will swivel and fire one of its three Skeets at it.

Weapons such as Skeet make it possible to combine the 'shotgun effect' with precision guidance, and hit groups of

Lasers have yet to prove themselves as practical weapons of air warfare rather than target ranging and designation systems. The US and Soviet Union have large scale directed energy weapons programmes and the USAF's ALL (Airborne Laser Laboratory) is one of the most dramatic results. A converted KC-135 was fitted with a carbon dioxide laser in a turret behind the cockpit with extensive test crew instrumentation (above and far left) and in tests managed to shoot down a drone and to burn a hole in a Sidewinder missile. There have been many proposals for making lasers practical tactical systems of offence or defence such as this USAF bomber with a tail mounted laser swatting down hostile missiles

small targets at relatively long range. Such weapons will be supported in service by aircraft-borne systems such as Joint Stars (stand-off target acquisition radar system), which is being developed to provide accurate, real-time targeting data for USAF and US Army stand-off missiles.

SUBMUNITIONS AND SMARTLETS

Submunitions can be delivered by a variety of vehicles; economically, this is a tremendous advantage. A single type of submunition can be produced for a variety of missiles, short-range and long-range, air-launched or surface-launched, increasing the production run and reducing costs. By the same token, a single basic type of missile, armed with different submunitions, can be used against a range of targets. Delivery systems can vary widely. In some British and German concepts, submunitions are ejected from a container attached to the aircraft. This has the advantage of delivering an extremely heavy load, but exposes the launch aircraft to defensive weapons. For the Advanced Tactical Fighter (ATF), the USAF is studying a gliding dispenser using lifting-body aerodynamics, and designed to blend with the carrier's aerodynamic configuration. This 'superconformal' weapon would reduce both drag and radar cross-section, and even without power it would have a stand-off range measured in miles. Advanced ground-launched systems based on submunitions include the awesome Lockheed Boss (ballistic offensive suppression system), a supersonic, delta-winged glider carrying a multi-ton load of submunitions and fired from a silo by a Trident missile booster. In the nearer term, the US Air Force and Army are studying a joint tactical missile (JTACMS) of the rocket-powered, semi-ballistic type, which could be launched from aircraft or land vehicles.

Modular concepts, mixing and matching widely produced components to a specific role, will extend to guidance systems. The Rockwell AGM-130, a rocket-boosted version of the GBU-15 gliding bomb, will have interchangeable laser homing or tv-tracking heads. Alternatively, future air-to-surface stand-off weapons might standardise on a mass-produced, low-cost laser inertial platform, which would be accurate enough to deliver submunitions within lethal distance.

Some air-launched tactical weapons will retain high-accuracy guidance systems and unitary warheads. They will include anti-tank missiles, which, like today's ATMs, will be common families of weapons to be carried by infantry, light armoured vehicles and helicopters. A consortium of French, German and British companies is working on two ATMs for the mid-1990s, under the designation Trigat (signifying third-generation anti-tank). One missile would be a medium-range, infantry-operated weapon with an unusual layout: it would have its motor in the front, thrusting through swivelling nozzles for initial lift and control, and the warhead in the rear. It is likely to be guided by a beam of infra-red light. In systems of this type, the launch post transmits a beam which constantly scans a pattern centred on the target. Sensors in the rear of the missile detect the beam as the scanning pattern passes over the missile, and the guidance system can then determine the missile's position within the beam, and direct it back towards the centre. The main advantages of optical beam-riding are that it is virtually impossible to jam or deceive; it also requires only a very small amount of equipment in the missile round, allowing the weight of the missile and the entire system to be minimised.

The long-range Trigat missile will meet different needs. Fire and forget is the watchword for such weapons, because of their longer flight time. Only an autonomous missile can free the launcher to engage another target or take evasive action while the first round is flying. Improved passive infra-red (IR) homing is the answer. The first IR homing systems could home only on to very-high-temperature sources such as aircraft jetpipes; if they were set to detect lower temperatures, they became too vulnerable to confusion by other objects in the field of view. Future IR units, however, will replace conventional optics by arrays of electronic sensors and high-power processing equipment; while they will not approach the imaging/target-recognition capability of the FLIR systems used by combat aircraft and sophisticated cruise missiles, they will be at once more sensitive and more discriminating than current weapons.

The long-range Trigat will be a 'top-attack' weapon, like most future ATMs. After launch, it will fly at a set altitude, sensing the proximity of the target and diving to hit its thinner top armour. Top-attack ATMs, made possible by more sophisticated guidance and fuzing systems, will become common in the next few years; they make it possible to destroy a tank with a smaller, lighter missile.

A completely different species of anti-tank weapon is the hypervelocity missile (HVM) under development by Vought. As its name suggests, the HVM's principal characteristic is high speed, in the region of Mach 4·5, obtained with a relatively large, high-energy motor. The missile needs no explosive warhead to destroy a tank; with an impact speed of nearly a mile per second, an assembly of metal rods will suffice. Flying almost a straight line to the target, the missile needs only a simple guidance system. For a fight time measured in seconds, the only control system needed is a pair of control ports fed with hot gas by small, electronically detonated explosive squibs. The result is that the missile is very small for its range and lethality, 20 rounds can be housed in a single pod, and a tactical fighter can carry several pods.

The HVM is guided by a laser radar system, somewhat simpler than a laser beam-riding device and capable of guiding multiple missiles. Sheer speed makes it possible to achieve multiple kills per pass, and like other optical beam-riders it is very difficult to jam.

The most difficult target for any air-launched missile, though, is another aircraft. Air-to-air missiles (AAMs) are excellent examples of the way in which reliable, compact and powerful electronic systems are changing the missile scene.

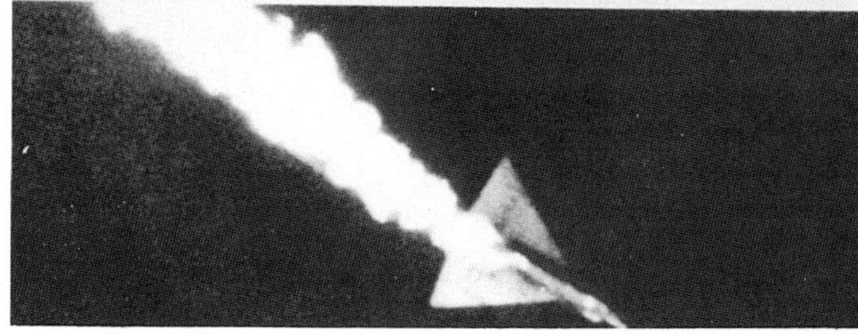

A Hughes AMRAAM (advanced Medium Range Air to Air Missile) launched from an F-16 shoots down a target drone. Unlike current generation medium range missiles such as the AIM-7 Sparrow, AMRAAM will be a true 'fire and forget system'

The biggest change over the rest of the 1980s will be the adoption of the Hughes AIM-120 Amraam (advanced medium-range AAM) as the standard weapon of Western air forces. With inertial mid-course guidance and active radar homing, AIM-120 significantly reduces the time during which the launch aircraft has to illuminate the target with its own radar.

Developments in combat aircraft in the 1990s will place increasing demands on the medium-range AAM. Targets will become stealthier, and their jamming systems more sophisticated. Engagements will take place at higher speeds and altitudes, and targets will be capable of manoeuvring at sustained supersonic speed. Some of these problems will be met by continued development of the guidance system. Future AAMs may incorporate memory-based guidance systems, for better

The ADATS missile seen below leaving its tracked launcher vehicle is a US-Swiss project for a highly accurate, all weather air defence/anti tank (ADATS) missile system. Target acquisition is by a combination of forward looking infra red, TV, radar and optical sight

discrimination between real targets and false images.

At the same time, there may be a major change in AAM propulsion. Most current AAMs are launched by a short-burn rocket motor, and on a long-distance interception they coast for much of the flight. Manoeuvring during the final phases of flight costs a great deal of energy, particularly at high altitudes where the small wings are inefficient. Ramjet propulsion is a potentially more efficient way of providing sustained power throughout the flight, and various types are being investigated for AAM propulsion. The traditional liquid-fuel ramjet is probably ruled out for the AAM by its complexity, as is the integral rocket/ramjet, in which rocket propellant packed inside the ramjet chamber is used to boost the missile to its cruising speed. Alternatives include solid-fuel ramjets, in which the air flows through the propellant, and the ducted rocket, which uses a solid-fuel gas generator to energise the ramjet. Some of these concepts are being studied for future AAMs, to replace Amraam and the US Navy's Phoenix.

The medium-range missile will still be backed up by a smaller, more agile weapon for short-range engagements; a European consortium is developing Asraam (advanced short-range AAM) for this role. Using improved IR guidance techniques, Asraam will be smaller and more compact than current weapons, and will be able to pull even tighter turns at high speed.

Development of destructive, precision-guided submunitions for air-to-surface weapons may alter the tactical missile balance to the disadvantage of the surface-to-air missiles (SAMs), particularly of the mobile, medium-range variety. These types necessarily rely on radar for detection and acquisition at medium ranges and low altitude, and this makes them prominent targets despite all the available counter-interception technology. (An example of this, and of its expense, is to fit each round with its own active radar guidance system.) Radar detection and location systems are being rapidly improved, good examples are the USAF's F-4G Wild Weasel, with its powerful onboard processing equipment, and the long-range precision emitter location system (PELS) carried by the TR-1. The same is true of anti-radar missiles. New weapons such as the US Harm and British Alarm are light enough to be carried for self-defence, and may be fast enough for the attacking aircraft to shoot it out with the SAM and win. Mobile missile launchers, radar vehicles and control vans are all large, soft targets; one cluster bomb can annihilate an entire battery. Once systems such as PELS and the joint stand-off missile are in service, an electromagnetic signature could turn into a suicide note.

The trend in land-based SAMs is likely to run towards shorter-range, faster-flying missiles, allowing quicker engagements and less time 'on the air'. Shorter-range weapons can also use passive means of detection, such as infra-red surveillance equipment, and low-probability-of-intercept guidance techniques such as laser beam-riding. An example of the trends in smaller SAMs is the Oerlikon/Martin-Marietta ADATS, a laser beam-riding weapon, some 50 per cent faster than current missiles in its class. It shows how smaller missiles are more easily built into protected vehicles; a complete ADATS system can be mounted on a single armoured vehicle, with eight rounds ready to fire. It is also an interesting example of the flexibility that is being built into modern missile systems thanks to miniaturisation, optical guidance and other technologies. ADATS is designed to attack tanks as well as aircraft, and is light enough to be adapted to helicopter launch.

Medium-range SAMs will retain their value for the defence of fixed, high-value targets such as airfields. It is possible that some will go underground for protection, and be vertically launched from silos. Vertical launch has already been adopted by the Soviet and British navies, because of its advantages in rate of fire, all-round defence and mechanical redundancy.

Naval SAMs are likely to develop differently from land-based weapons. Better protected, and accordingly designed with fewer concerns about the risks of detection, they will continue to be developed as successively more lethal, accurate and cunning anti-ship missiles make their appearance. One US Navy study concerns an 'outer air battle' SAM, intended to engage Soviet *Backfires* before they could release their own missiles. It would be a costly weapon, almost certainly with a fire-and-forget active radar guidance system and extensive counter-jamming capability, and powered by a ramjet engine, but its use would mean intercepting one large target rather than three smaller and equally lethal vehicles.

In the later 1990s, shorter-range naval SAMs could be on the point of replacement by radically new technologies such as the laser and the hypervelocity railgun. Different technologies, these have some common attributes: very high speed, limited range at low altitude, and a large power requirement which will make them less likely to be used in highly mobile applications. Initially, they may be more suited to shipboard use, particularly in the anti-missile role, than to land.

Cheap expendable systems such as the Israeli Aircraft Industries Scout surveillance drones will have as much impact on the face of warfare as supersophisticated systems. Scout drones can transmit TV pictures in real time to remote operators allowing them to see the landscape over which it is travelling

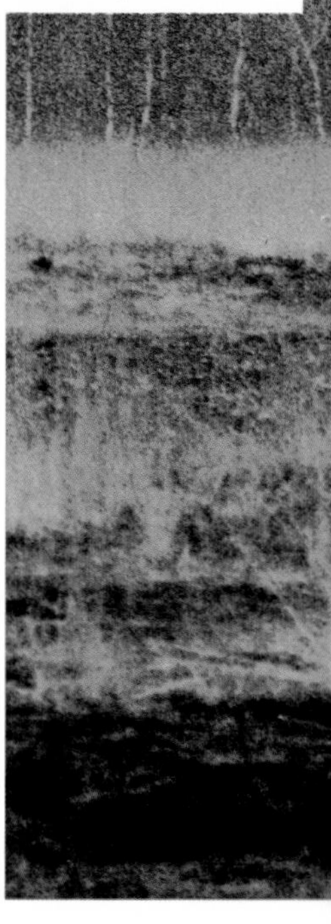

Right: Canadair AN/USD-501 reconnaissance drone launch. Like the Scout, the USD-501 flies over hostile territory but returns with photographic or infrared linescan intelligence. Beyond such 'remotely piloted vehicles' are Unmanned Military Vehicles guided by advanced computers with a degree of artificial intelligence which may supplant the manned aircraft in some roles

The conventional missile will lose none of its importance to the land, sea or air battle, but it will be joined in increasing numbers by a new race of unmanned military air vehicles, falling somewhere between the traditional 'drone' or RPV and the missile itself. Currently, these UVSs are at a very early stage of their evolution. They are controversial in military circles, and often encounter opposition among air force commanders, virtually all of whom are ex-pilots. It is also argued that one of the main advantages of the UVS, cost, may diminish or disappear when the original concept is adapted into something of any military usefulness.

The term UVS is used, rather than RPV, because most of the new systems are not 'remotely piloted'. Instead; they are flown by their own pre-programmed navigation and flight control systems. Some of them can be commanded to change

their destination in flight, but they do not need a full-time pilot. Others have no means for human intervention at all.

High-performance UVSs were extensively used for reconnaissance during the Vietnam war, but for a number of reasons, some political and some economic, their use was sharply reduced in the mid-1970s; the Soviet Union still uses a Mach 2·8 reconnaissance UVS, and some covert US units may still maintain such systems on strength. Most attention, though, has switched to far smaller, much less complicated machines. These saw their first use in combat in 1982, when the Israeli Defence Forces used Scout and Mastiff UVSs to reconnoitre Syrian positions.

Reconnaissance is one of the prime role for the UVS, and one in which it will be increasingly used. Barely larger than an enthusiast's flying model, the UVS is virtually impossible to shoot down, and yet it can carry a stabilised, steerable tv camera and transmission equipment and send instant tv images to the 'consumers' at the front of the battle. The US Army's Aquila, similar to the Israeli systems, but somewhat more sophisticated, more automated and more expensive, will be developed with a night-reconnaissance capability, and carries a laser to mark targets for guided artillery shells. The British Phoenix system will perform a similar task. By the 1990s, reconnaissance UVSs will be established in service with most ground forces.

The second mission to be performed by an operational UVS is the suppression of hostile electronic warfare (EW) equipment. In 1983, the USAF unveiled an extraordinary machine called Pave Tiger. Many details of the system are classified, but it is known that Pave Tiger was developed in considerable

Lockheed Aquila launch and recovery sequence. This US Army RPV has great tactical significance, not only as a surveillance system but as a target designation platform and for directly attacking hostile radar and communications networks

haste, to deal with a new and very effective ground-based Soviet EW system.

Pave Tiger is based on a Boeing-developed canard airframe, weighing 250 lb, injection-moulded in foamed plastic and glassfibre, and powered by a cheap commercial piston engine driving a small plastic propeller. Fifteen of these 'air vehicles' can be stowed in separate cells in a module the size of a standard freight container, each attached to its individual launch rail. The module is attached to a standard power unit and a control box; the vehicles pop out of their cells on demand and take off on a pre-programmed track, loaded before launch from the control unit.

Details of the mission and payload of Pave Tiger are classified, but it appears to be what is known as a 'harassment' system. A homing device picks up emissions from the system to be suppressed, and the vehicle, which carries an explosive charge, begins an attack run towards it. The operators respond by shutting down their transmissions. Instead of crashing like an ordinary missile, though, the UVS abandons its attack and begins to orbit the target, circling for hours and diving to the attack should tbe operators restart the system. One small drone can paralyse a highly sophisticated EW system for hours, at far less cost than the short-term supression achieved by an airstrike.

Pave Tiger will be acquired in thousands. Systems like it can saturate hostile airspace with hundreds of buzzing plastic insects, virtually unswattable and equipped with lethal stings. Modular philosophies will help keep production costs down; the airframe, flight controls and transport/launch system used in Pave Tiger can be used to carry almost any electronic/munitions payload.

The expendable airframe and the launch system used for the Pave Tiger mission has also been developed with an eye to naval applications. Compact, zero-maintenance UVSs have many potential uses at sea; chaff-bombing and jamming to deceive missiles, over-the-horizon, covert electronic surveillance and communications relay.

Higher-performance UVSs can also be used to deceive SAMs; it was reported that this was done in the air battles over the Lebanon in 1982. A wave of UVSs went in ahead of the main strike force and absorbed the first barrage of SAMs, and the operators were still reloading when the strike force arrived. Such a simple tactic might be less effective against a better organised opposition, but deception UVSs will probably become more subtle and sophisticated in time.

Another emerging UVS class is the high-altitude, very-long-endurance type. In the 1990s, this could emerge as the

replacement for aircraft such as the U-2/TR-1, carrying sensors and relay equipment; eliminating the pilot would improve performance, cost, endurance and productivity. Lockheed has revealed a design study for a 267-foot span UVS, powered by convertible fan/shaft engines driving 40-foot propellers. The two-blade propellers would be stopped for take-off, climb and landing, and the engines would run as turbofans; they would switch into shaft-drive mode in the cruise, to optimise propulsive efficiency. The aircraft would have an endurance measured in days.

An alternative means of accomplishing the same mission is the microwave-powered aircraft. A ground station would transmit a high-power microwave beam to the electrically-powered UVS, which would have a pick-up system called a rectenna (rectifier/antenna) built into the lower skin of its wing. The aircraft would probably operate on a 'boost-glide' basis, gliding for several hours and returning to the vicinity of the ground station to climb back to peak cruising height. Other approaches to the long-endurance mission include solar-powered aircraft, although such sytems are severely hampered by winter and extreme latitudes, or airships; Lockheed has studied UVSs of both types at various times.

Of all aerospace systems, satellites and UVSs will benefit the most from the development of artificial intelligence, and its implementation in lightweight VHSIC-based electronic equipment. Intelligence is hard to define, but one example illustrates its potential to military missions. Current UVSs can act according to sensor information, or according to a pre-programmed set of instructions. An 'intelligent' UVS will be able to do both at once. A future tactical reconnaissance UVS, for example, will be crossing country at high speed on a programmed track when its wide-angle, scanning infra-red sensor detects a vehicle. IR instantly cues long-focus optical and other sensors, and target-recognition identifies a tank. The UVS turns, returns to the same spot using its inertial reference system, and makes a low-altitude run over the tank's projected track, revealing the entire formation. The UVS's memory tells it that the formation is very significant, and its datalink promptly transmits high-resolution images to an orbiting high-altitude relay UVS behind friendly lines.

Combining intelligence with immediate action, such a UVS will have become a true robot. Note that it does not require a human operator in such a high-risk situation; the reduced size of the unmanned vehicle further increases its chances of survival. Neither does it saturate the data-link with high-quality images of passing trees. The technology envisaged is not far from reality, but at present such data processing can only be combined with action in a 'stop-think-move' cycle. It may be very different in the 1990s; and it is not hard to envisage the UVS carrying Skeets or similar weapons in place of some of its sensors. At that point, the missile and the UVS may become almost impossible to tell apart.

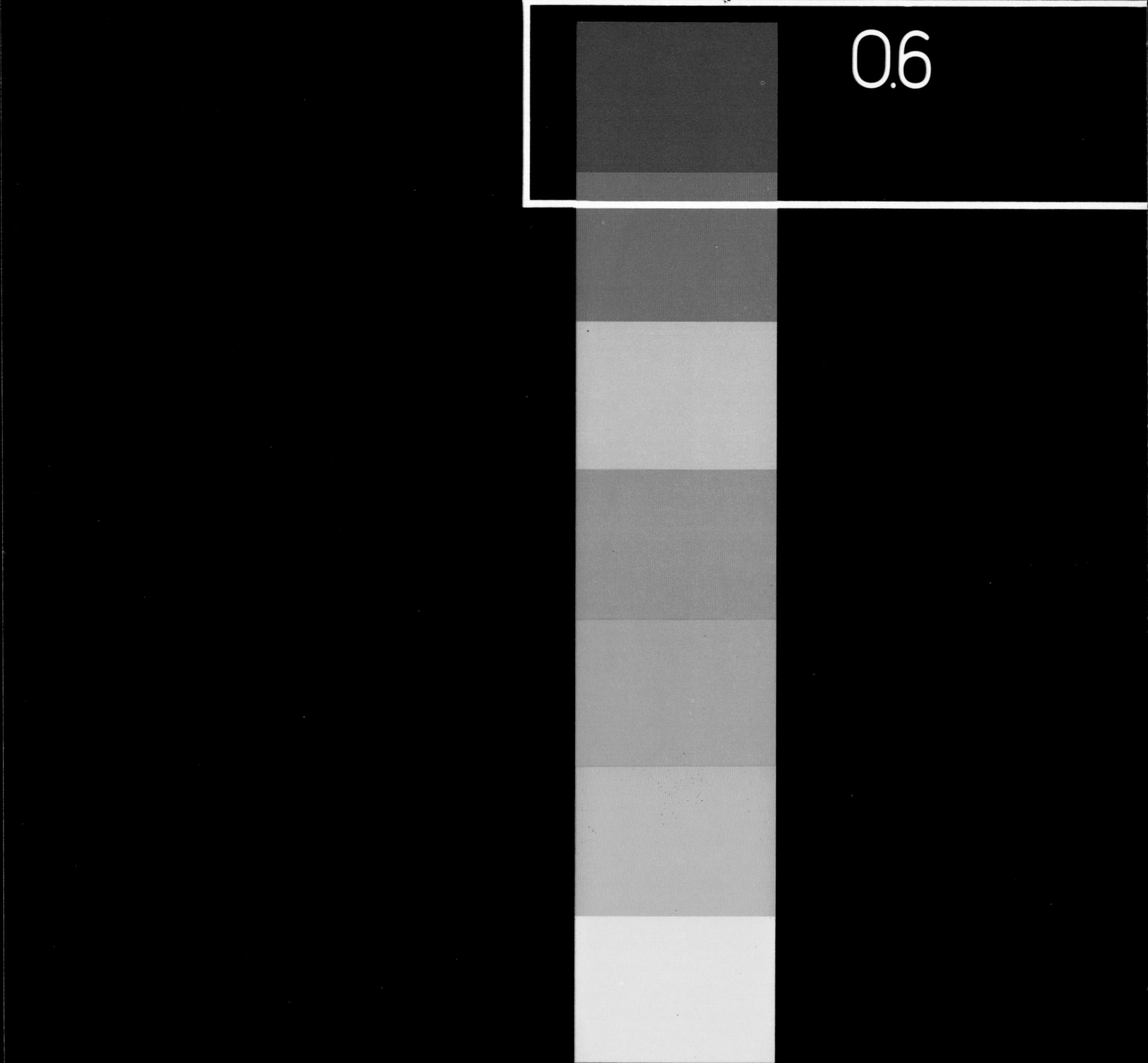
0.6

People Movers

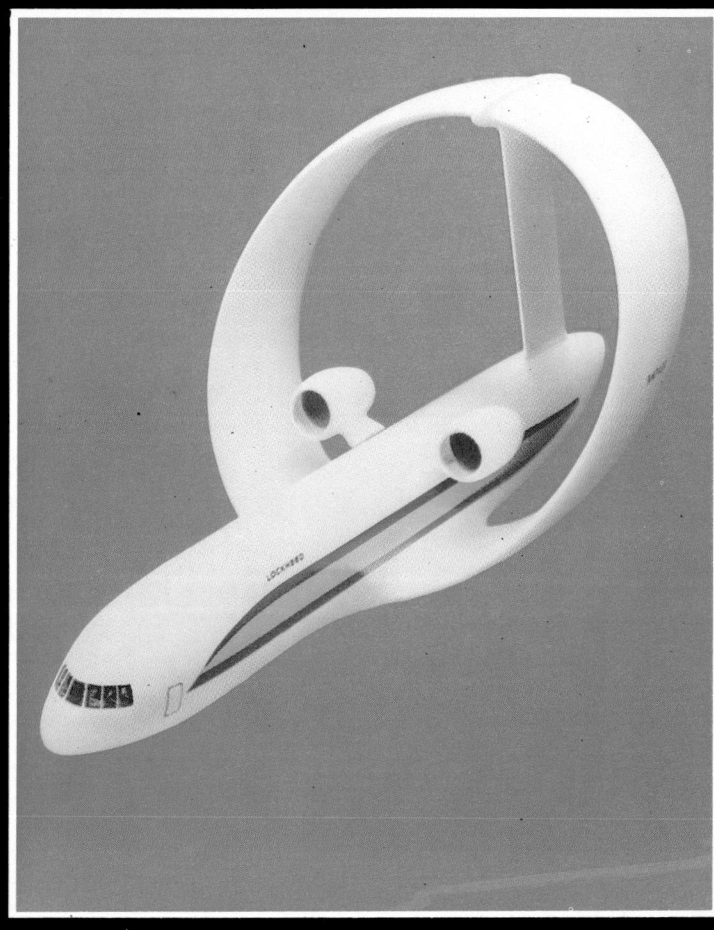

Lockheed's proposal for a ringwing airliner

By far the greater part of the world's population has never travelled by air, a simple fact that is sometimes overlooked by prosperous Western Europeans and North Americans. This is not to say that all of them ever will, just that the airline industry still has room to grow.

The development of the airline industry is in some ways a sociological phenomenon. While what the industry does can influence the way people travel, cheap charter flights were the key to persuading Europeans to take their holidays abroad, for example, its fortunes also depend on how much money people have to spend, and whether they find other things to spend it on. Business travel is different, but it fills only a minority of airline seats.

Successful airlines in the year 2000 will be the ones that have responded to the demands of the market in one way or another. Today, it is possible to see two emerging types of airline, certainly among the operators of larger aircraft, where the stakes and potential winnings are higher. Some are developing into highly efficient organisations with generally low costs. They have modern aircraft, no more management staff than they need, and make the greatest possible use of information systems to help their people do their jobs efficiently. The result is that they can quickly adapt their product to suit changing market conditions or different markets. The better European or Far Eastern airlines, and some of the big US carriers, fall into that category.

The other major type of airline is the specialist operator, serving a single region, or a single market sector, and achieving efficiency by concentrating on that market. In this type of operation, costs are low because lines of communication are short, the staff is small and highly motivated and operations are concentrated at relatively few points. Success in marketing depends on knowing the area of operations

Great white hope of the European airliner industry is the 150-seat Airbus A320 designed to compete one key sector at least with the US aerospace giants

better than any outsider. Examples of specialised airlines range from commuter operators serving a single city to the low-cost charter operators in Europe, some of which are quite large. In a related category are the express-parcels services pioneered in the United States.

The sick airlines of today are the carriers which have not yet fallen into either of these categories. They include specialists which have tried to expand into new and unfamiliar markets, without the strength and resources at the disposal of big, flexible carriers. At the other end of the spectrum are major carriers which have over-extended themselves into markets well served by specialists, and have accordingly found themselves fighting many small wars of attrition. Both classes will either have to reform their ideas or face inevitable decline.

What devices will airline managements use in the year 2000? One thing is certain, then, as now, an airline's most important asset will be its people. An airline's business does not deal with assembling parts and raw materials into products, but with using machinery to produce a service. Inevitably, this means that the airline's people are basic to the success of the operation. They need not only to be paid, but also to be managed, insured, given room to work and provided with means and channels to communicate with each other.

It follows that the current arguments about airline pay scales, which are very active in the USA and will certainly spread to the rest of the Western world, are virtually irrelevant. An airline can hire twice as many people to do the same work as its rival, at half the hourly wage, and will still bear all those additional costs as well as the inefficiency inherent in overstaffing. Productivity, not pay, is what matters.

An airline's people work in separate bases hundreds or thousands of miles apart. Information, at that point, is not simply important, it is the organisation's nervous system, and there will be no room for dinosaur reflexes in the year 2000. Fortunately, it is precisely that area which has seen the greatest advances in technological history, and which will continue to do so in the next decade.

The first computer terminals which many people saw were in travel agents' offices or behind airline check-in desks;

767
BOEING 767
757
BOEING 757
N757A

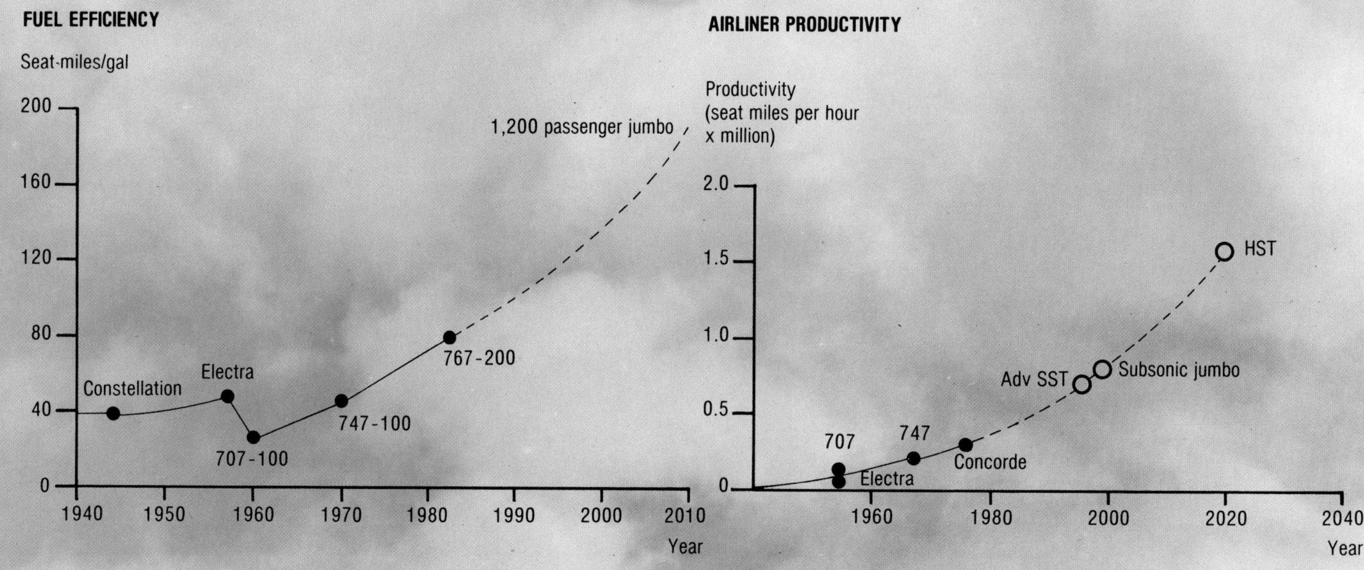

FUEL EFFICIENCY
Seat-miles/gal
200
160
120
80
40
0
1,200 passenger jumbo
Constellation
Electra
707-100
747-100
767-200
1940
1950
1960
1970
1980
1990
2000
2010
Year
AIRLINER PRODUCTIVITY
Productivity (seat miles per hour x million)
2.0
1.5
1.0
0.5
0
HST
Adv SST
Subsonic jumbo
707
747
Electra
Concorde
1960
1980
2000
2020
2040
Year

Left: In the late 1970s Boeing hedged its bets on the future shape of airline operations by announcing two new airliners, the narrow bodied 757 and the longer range, shorter, wide bodied 767. Fuel efficiency over appropriate ranges is the touchstone of airliner design, with Boeing locked in deadly battle with European contenders such as the Airbus 310 (right) and Airbus 320. These aircraft will still be the airline workhorses of the year 2000 and their replacements are likely to differ outwardly only in detail

Left below: These charts show how fuel efficiency and airliner productivity can go on improving beyond the year 2000. NASA foresees that a 1200 passenger superjumbo would double present seat-miles flown per gallon of fuel while increases both in capacity and speed would keep the productivity curve climbing upwards

airlines were quick to adapt the computer to their reservations systems. Behind the scenes, airlines have also been major users of computers and information systems. These, though, will see improvements in speed and power over the next decade or so. It is now technically possible, for example, for an aircraft's on-board test and diagnosis computers to analyse many systems malfunctions, identifying the faulty component while the aircraft is still in flight. That information can be transferred directly to the engineering department, the nearest replacement part to the aircraft's destination can be located immediately, and the spare can be on its way to the destination before the aircraft has landed.

Some 'factory of the future' technologies could also find uses in the airline industry. Using a portable terminal, for example, a technician could consult the complete manual for the aircraft system under study, obtain the part number needed and order it delivered to his work station. Computerised information transfer, combined with the international expansion of high-speed package services, will enable airlines to reduce their stocks of expensive spares.

Airline route systems will also be structured to reduce costs. Interestingly, the pattern that was forced on European airlines by national fragmentation is also the most economical for an individual company: a single main base, from which services radiate like the spokes of a wheel. 'Hub-and-spoke' systems allow middle-sized cities to be served without adding unattractive 'milk-run' stops on long-distance services. They allow maintenance and flight operations activities to be concentrated at the hubs, where nearly all the airline's flights either arrive or depart. Small teams, or subcontracted agents, are sufficient to handle the airline's needs at the ends of the spokes.

Hub-and-spoke systems have a number of implications. They provide one-stop service between many points, but tend to cut down on the most convenient non-stop service. They generate opportunities for the smallest airlines; by concentrating a great deal of long-haul traffic and service at a single point, a major airline hub creates demand for all kinds of services into that hub, such as commuter and helicopter flights. Meanwhile, on the rim of the hub-and-spoke system, some city pairs may lose the direct services they once enjoyed, and smaller airlines may move in to fill the gap. An increasing number of major airlines are now recognising this situation, and reaching agreements with smaller carriers to co-operate in serving the hub area.

Outside the USA, most airlines will continue to be single-hub operators, because few states will give a foreign airline the right to schedule a flight to any final destination other than its own country. Even in the United States, though, it will take a very large airline to operate more than one hub successfully.

Maintaining an efficient hub-and-spoke network, with its attendant feeder services, will call for a very careful tailoring of aircraft size to the length and density of the route to be flown. Through the co-operation between large airlines and small regional or commuter carriers, the new pattern of the airline industry will eliminate any clear boundaries between 'trunk', 'regional' and 'commuter' airlines. The industry will need a complete range of aircraft types, and the forces of the market will ensure that there are no large gaps in capacity or performance to be filled.

The basic characteristics of airliners will be defined by the same considerations as they are today. Long distances and large aircraft will still go together, generally speaking; the demand for frequency and convenience is less important, and the superior economics of the larger aircraft more significant. Short-haul services demand more frequent flights from a

greater range of locations, and hence smaller aircraft are more common. On short sectors, proportionally more time is spent taxiing, climbing or descending, and aircraft speed is less significant in terms of the time taken from departure gate to arrival gate; therefore, short-haul aircraft may tend to be slower. Lastly, because short-haul services need to reach a greater number of airports, the aircraft used will tend to have better runway performance.

Operating costs will be the key to an airline's choice among competing aircraft types, just as they are today. Improved fuel efficiency is something which airlines now demand with every new subtype which the manufacturers introduce, and still greater advances are promised by design features now under test. But maintenance costs, particularly in the powerplant, will also be important for any new commercial aircraft.

FUEL EFFICIENCY

Concerns about the future supply of aviation fuel have receded somewhat since the early 1970s. Conservation measures have slowed and in some cases reversed the rise in the use of hydrocarbon fuels. These were largely driven by the politically accelerated rise of fuel prices, but showed the effectiveness of price as a conservation tool. It is now accepted that aviation's needs for hydrocarbons can be met for the rest of the century without resorting to shale or synthetics. The advanced development of systems to use such alternative sources of fuel could be an issue by the year 2000, and might provoke a re-examination of other types of fuel. Neither is there much doubt that fuel will continue to get more expensive over the long term, despite short-term gluts and slumps.

Another factor should be considered when assessing the likely shape of the airline industry, and of the aircraft which it will use, in the year 2000: the potential development of alternative modes of transport, such as high-speed trains. Cruising around 200 mph, such vehicles are certainly capable of equalling the speed of air travel between two city centres, over a quite considerable distance, and without the inconvenience of travelling to an out-of-town airport. They use limited quantities of cheap energy and are very safe. The trains themselves can be built more cheaply than aircraft of the same size, but the construction and maintenance of track represents a daunting investment.

While high-speed trains may prove to be effective competition for air travel, the chances are that they will do so only in a few markets satisfying some or all of a number of conditions: a large traffic flow, inconveniently placed or congested airports, available surface access to an attractive city centre, and so on. Even so, serious planing would have to start today for a future high-speed surface link to be complete by the year 2000. Hardware would need to be selected, environmental questions answered and the initial investment raised. It is probably fair to say that a 250 mph, 500-mile rail link would cost as much to build as a brand-new, high-technology short-haul airliner would cost to develop; the same up-front investment would pave the way to linking one city pair by train, or thousands of city pairs by aircraft. Under such circumstances, backers are likely to be somewhat sceptical.

With that in mind, the first thing to be said about the airliners of the year 2000 is that many of them can be seen at the world's airports today. First-generation jetliners such as the 707 and DC-8 have lasted about 20 years in service before becoming technologically obsolete, or before their structures began to need so much attention that repairs were uneconomical. Stretched DC-8s, already 13–14 years old, are being put through re-engining programmes in the expectation of

Right: The Lear Fan 2100 was the first corporate aircraft to make extensive use of carbonfibre reinforced plastic, in fact only the engines and undercarriage legs are made of metal. New airliners are flying routinely with composite fins, control surfaces and fairings but the all-composite big airliner is still a long way off.
Left: Weight reduction through new materials is one component of fuel efficiency while propfans offer another over certain ranges. This is a mock-up of the Fokker 50 advanced turboprop short-haul transport

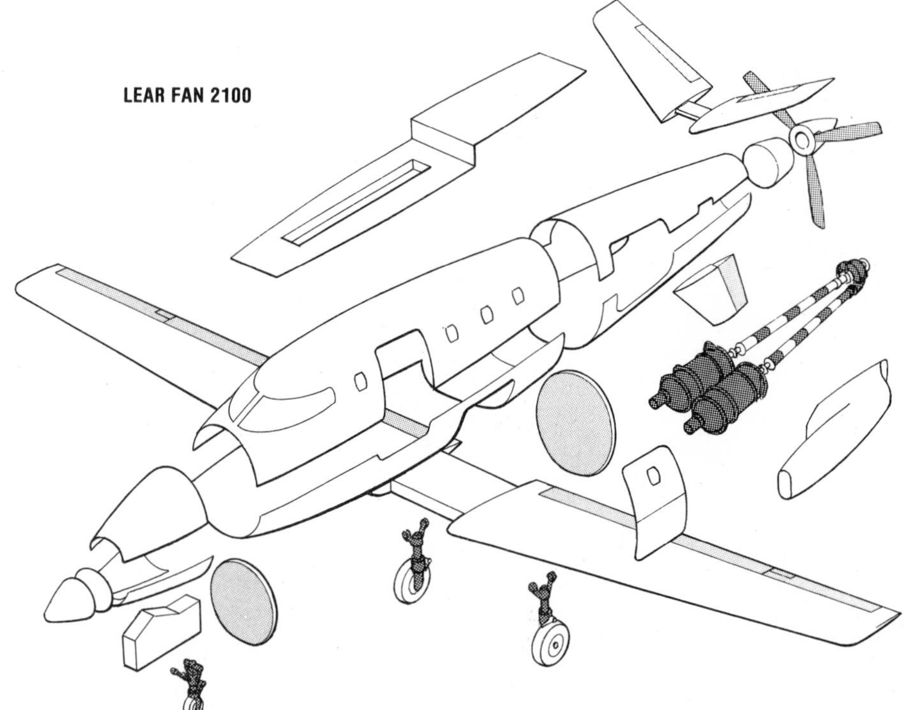

Carbon fibre reinforced plastic (CFRP)
CFRP sandwich
Kevlar reinforced plastic
Metal

another ten years' lease of life. The BAC One-Elevens delivered to the United States in the mid-1960s are still going strong on punishing, high-frequency short-haul operations. The wide-body jets represented a useful advance in structural technology, using more machined-from-the-solid components, more bonding and more efficient structural designs and, so far, none of them has shown evidence of any appreciable airframe wear. If the DC-8 can last 25 years, the wide-bodies should be good for 30–35 years at least, and possibly more. This would mean that every one of the 1000-plus wide-bodies built to date will still be flyable in the year 2000, and a good proportion of them will have five to ten years' flying left in them.

Looking back once again at the first generation of jets, it is possible to predict with a fair degree of certainty that even the earliest wide-body jets will be far from obsolescent in the year 2000. New aircraft such as the Boeing 767 and A310 should still be in production. They differ from their immediate predecessors mainly in having improved engines and much improved electronics, and all such components can be replaced. A 'mid-life update' programme would produce an aircraft with new-technology features and operating costs, and costing about half as much per seat as a new aircraft. The aircraft manufacturers themselves are most unlikely to initiate such a development, because it competes directly with their bread-and-butter business of building airframes. Nearly all the price of a rehabilitated jet such as the DC-8 Super 70 goes to the engine and subsystem manufacturers. Instead, such work is likely to be organised by independent contractors, with funding from the suppliers, as was done with the DC-8 programme.

Some major airlines have acquired DC-8 Super 70s, raising the possibility that many of the world's bigger airlines, the manufacturers' prime customers, might choose such a mid-life update in favour of buying new aircraft as their current wide-body aircraft begin to age. This could significantly reduce the demand for new aircraft by the mid-1990s, and, because of low production rates, new aircraft could be more expensive.

As noted earlier, it is a safe prediction that many current types of aircraft will still be coming off the assembly lines in the year 2000, for reasons of both economics and technology. Historically, it has taken at least ten years of production for a commercial aircraft programme to show a useful profit, and most successful programmes have run for at least 20 years. Conversely, continuing the development of an existing aircraft saves an enormous investment in the design of a brand-new type.

Switching to a replacement aircraft in the same category only makes sense if it is the only way to take full advantage of new technology, and if that new technology offers enough of an improvement to offset the development costs. While it is nearly always possible to incorporate new technology in a derivative aircraft, an all-new type will tend to make better use of it. The design of an airliner involves a careful balance of characteristics, wing area and span, seating and fuel capacity, runway and climb performance, and so on, which combine to optimise the aircraft to the needs of the average operator. When a design is extensively modified, this balance is distorted and the economics and performance usually suffer.

When Boeing decided to develop the 767 to replace the 727, a new aircraft was the only way to incorporate new wing aerodynamics, and new structural techniques, along with an efficient installation for the best engines available. The most likely candidate for a launch decision as these words are written is the Airbus A320, to which similar considerations apply. The A320, together with any comparable aircraft from

Boeing, is designed to replace the 737 and DC-9, the last members of the first generation of jets developed in 1958–65, and the last jets designed to use low-bypass turbofan engines.

CONVENTIONAL BUT EFFICIENT

Will it be possible to make economic sense of a replacement for the current wide-body jets, between now and the year 2000? Increased capacity alone is unlikely to justify such a development; the airline industry is likely to grow at a slower, steadier pace in the 1980s and 1990s than in the formative years of the 1960s. The question is whether technology will advance far enough to threaten the current generation with obsolescence, and repay the $2000 million development costs of a brand-new high-capacity airliner. Aerodynamics, structures, propulsion and electronics all offer some room for improvement, but will it be enough?

Radical aerodynamic configurations offer fewer benefits to airliners than to military or personal aircraft. The 767/A310 configuration, with two engines under a swept wing and the tail aft, may seem conventional and unimaginative, but in fact is a refined and efficient configuration for a large airliner. Canard or three-surface layouts are appealing for business aircraft; they eliminate trim drag, the result of the constant downforce generated by a conventional tailplane, and allow the use of more efficient pusher propellers and mid-set wings. These considerations simply do not apply to an airliner. Trim drag can be reduced by the simpler expedient of increasing the authority of the flight control system, making smaller stability margins acceptable, and by using a rear-fuselage fuel tank for trim, a technique pioneered on Concorde and revived for the long-range version of the A310. The conventional airliner engine installation is efficient, it spreads the weight of the aircraft along the wing, reducing stresses on the structure, and presents no control problems, because the engines are relatively close to the centreline. The engines and the fuel load are close to the centre of gravity, making the aircraft tolerant of different loadings. The powerplants are also at a very convenient height for maintenance. Finally, a mid-set wing offers few advantages to a large airliner, because the fuselage cross-

Above: The high speed turboprop, alias the propfan, features eight or ten thin, swept blades and is designed to operate at speeds up to Mach 0.8 absorbing power up to 10,000 hp. The propfan is a significant development in prospect for civil aircraft or tactical military transports (above right) but it produces the highest efficiency gains at very short or very long ranges.

Left: A British contender in the short haul high efficiency turboprop powered airliner of the future market is the British Aerospace ATP based on the HS 748 airframe

section with a large diameter and a flat floor naturally provides plenty of room for the wing to pass through the body. Very little detailed study of radical configurations for large airliners has been undertaken so far. Such work could be under way in the 1990s, but it is unlikely to lead to a production programme by the year 2000.

Very similar considerations apply to structures for large aircraft. Once again, radical departures from current technology are more difficult to justify for airliners than for other types of aircraft. For example, one of the principal attractions of carbon-fibre composite material is that it is stiff, as well as strong. For smaller aircraft stiffness is important because it is the essence of good handling, but the metal structure of a large airliner has just about the right 'give' for its mission. It does not need to endure high air loads, because airliners fly slowly in the thicker air of low altitudes, and its resilience is the key to its durability.

The application of composite material to the 'primary structure', wing skins and spars, pressure hull and empennage, of a large airliner will require some very detailed investigation in at least three areas. One of them, as indicated above, is the design of large, low-airspeed composite structures. Another is the manufacture of large components: it is hard to envisage an autoclave large enough to cure a 747 skin panel, for example. But perhaps the biggest area of uncertainty is life. Most military and personal aircraft fly for only a few hundred hours every year; airliners fly thousands of hours, and a short-haul airliner may make that many take-offs and landings, which are the toughest part of the airframe's life.

Meanwhile, the metallurgists have struck back with aluminium-lithium (Al-Li) alloys. Lithium is the lightest of all the metals, and its effect is to create an alloy which is less dense than current materials, somewhat stiffer and equally strong. The fact that the improved strength/weight ratio is achieved through lower density, rather than higher tensile strength, makes the use of Al-Li particularly attractive; in theory, the new material could simply be substituted for conventional aluminium without changing any measurements or gauges (a wing panel, for instance, could be fabricated on a machine tool, using the same control program). The component would be visually identical to the conventional part, and mechanically interchangeable with it, but would be ten per cent lighter. In the case of components where stiffness is important, such as control surfaces, the weight benefit could be up to 20 per cent.

Development of Al-Li alloys is now well under way. Currently, it is considered too great a technical risk to incorporate the new material throughout the structure, and the switch to Al-Li will be gradual. The first alloy of the type to be approved for aircraft use is likely to be a general-purpose alloy, which accounts for 30–40 per cent of the aluminium in a large civil aircraft and is used for forgings, extrusions and less-stressed components. Airbus Industrie predicts that general-purpose aluminium-lithium will be available in time for the A320, to enter service in mid-1988. This material will be followed by a high-strength alloy, for such components as wing top skins, and the last of the group to appear (because it requires the most exhaustive test and evaluation) will be a fatigue-resistant alloy for wing lower skins and fuselage skins. It will be the early to mid-1990s before production airliners can use Al-Li throughout the structure. As noted earlier, it should be quite easy to incorporate the new material in existing aircraft. Aluminium-lithium, therefore, is one new technology which will prolong, rather than shorten, the production lives of current designs.

In only one area of airliner technology are radical changes attracting a great deal of attention and that is powerplants.

Simply, the reason for this is that the engine is where the fuel is burnt; fuel has been steadily rising in price over the past decade, and is expected to continue doing so. An improvement in propulsion efficiency can be directly related to a cut in operating costs, and this is guaranteed to win the customer's attention. Radical innovations are now under study, because the present line of evolution appears to be near an end.

REFINED BIG-FANS

Refined versions of the current big-fans engines still offer useful improvements in fuel consumption, and will retain their full performance throughout their service lives. High-efficiency compressors, wide-chord fan blades and fully electronic controls bring significant benefits, and will be standard on most engines by the 1990s. Pratt & Whitney's current plans are typical of the way this gradual development will be managed. P&W is now delivering the first of its all-new PW2037 engines; meanwhile, experience gained with the PW2037 is making it possible to incorporate further improved technology in the PW4000, a new engine in a larger size class. In a few years' time, the company will introduce a developed version of the PW2037, which will incorporate and improve on PW4000 technology in exactly the same way.

But the big-fan engine has built-in limitations, and some major changes will be needed to repeat the sort of efficiency improvements which came with its original introduction. An aircraft powerplant has two vital qualities, its thermodynamic efficiency, which defines how well it turns fuel into mechanical energy, and its propulsive efficiency, or the effectiveness with which it uses that energy to drive the aircraft. The two are not always compatible in a simple powerplant. High thermodynamic efficiency means using the highest possible pressure and temperature ratios; propulsive efficiency involves matching the speed of the propulsive jet to the speed of the aircraft.

In a pure jet engine, the speed of the exhaust jet rises as the pressure ratio rises, because there is more energy in the exhaust. With currently achievable pressure ratios, the pure jet can achieve good propulsive efficiency at quite high supersonic speeds. The original low-bypass turbofan was designed to bring the exhaust stream velocity closer to transport speeds. As the pressure ratio of the core was increased, more energy was extracted from the core stream, through a multi-stage low-pressure turbine, to drive a much larger fan. This was the rationale for the high-bypass engine.

The problem now is that there are limits to the development of the conventional high-bypass engine. If the core pressure ratio is increased, there is more power to drive the fan; but if the fan diameter is constant, the result will be a faster fan exhaust, and propulsive efficiency will actually be reduced. If the fan diameter is significantly increased, though, it will have to be driven by a larger turbine. Because the torque loads on the shaft are greater, it must be increased in diameter as well. At the same time, presumably, the high-pressure-ratio core is reduced in size, and the problems of mechanical and aerodynamic mismatching rapidly get out of hand.

The basic answer to the problem is to break up the intimate relationship between the basic gas turbine engine, the core, and the propulsion subsystem. A partial step is to gear the fan to the low-pressure turbine, allowing the latter to be designed for greater speeds and higher efficiency, but the design of such a gearbox for a 40 000 lb engine would be no small task. Rolls-Royce has studied a 'geared, mid-fan' engine in which the fan is mounted behind the core, and driven by two turbine stages, a high-speed geared stage and a slower direct-drive stage.

Propulsion systems made up of a discrete gas turbine and propulsor, connected by a geared transmission, have been around for almost as long as the jet engine; they are called turboprops. They are very efficient, much more so than high-bypass fan engines, but their use has been limited mainly by speed. Most propellers begin to experience sharply declining efficiency at Mach 0·6, much less than the speed of a jet airliner. In the mid-1970s, as fuel costs began to mount, US designers began work on a propulsion system which can either be considered as a high-speed propeller, or as a very-high-bypass turbofan with its cowling removed to save weight. Appropriately, it is called the propfan.

The propfan could be a very significant development in aircraft propulsion, offering a 20 per cent improvement in efficiency over a conventional fan using comparable technology. It has been made possible by composite materials and supercritical aerodynamics. Being a radical development, it raises a number of technical questions, and current work is aimed at finding answers.

PROPELLER COMEBACK

Conventional propellers are limited to Mach 0·6 or so because the tips of the blades travel along a helical path through the air, at a higher speed than the aircraft itself. At speeds above Mach 0·6, the tips of the blades begin to approach the speed of sound. Propeller blades built in metal must be slender, and quite thick, to withstand the loads to which they are subjected, and their aerofoils tend to have poor transonic characteristics. The result is a rapid decline in efficiency at high speed. The propfan blade, though, is built from stiff composite materials using aeroelastic tailoring techniques, giving the designer a great deal more freedom. It has a thin section, like a transonic wing, and advanced aerodynamic technology is used to create sections which have good transonic efficiency. The propfan blade is sweptback, to further improve transonic behaviour; the sweep angle is increased gradually from the root to the tip, where the rotational velocity is highest, giving it its characteristic scimitar planform.

The other key element of the propfan design is the use of eight or ten blades, twice as many as most conventional propellers. The primary reason for this is to reduce the diameter. Propellers designed using conventional disc loadings (the ratio of power to propeller diameter) are inconveniently large for high-powered transonic aircraft, calling for engines to be placed too far outboard, stalky and heavy landing gears and other weight-increasing features. Reducing the diameter of the propeller tends to overwork the blades, and reduces their efficiency; increasing the number of blades both recoups some of the lost efficiency and, by reducing the load on each blade, makes structural design easier.

The next major step in propfan development is to fly a pair of near-full-size units, probably on the wings of a rear-engined

The cockpit of the Airbus A. 310 represents the state of the art in airliner flight control layout with its large multi-function displays, but still relies on traditional dial instruments and switching. The airliner cockpit of the future will show increasing use of computerised flat screen and head up displays and even greater ergonomic economy in hands-on controls

jet such as a Gulfstream II. Propfan technology issues include the effects of a high-speed, swirling slipstream on the airframe, and the possibility that it could generate very high interference drag. The noise and vibration characteristics of a transonic propeller, both inside and outside the aircraft, will also be investigated; noise and vibration are two of the least predictable qualities of any aircraft system, and the only thing that is certain about the propfan's characteristics is that they will be unique. Another problem area is the transmission. Western expertise in reliable turboprop transmissions runs to 6000 shp powerplants, but even a 100-seat transonic twin-engined airliner will need at least twice as much power per engine. Moreover, the problems of gearbox design tend to increase out of proportion to the engine's output. The transmission of a 40 000 shp wide-body engine beggars comprehension, and will call for technology that is not even identified.

There are a number of solutions on offer. Airframe interaction and internal noise could be practically eliminated with a pusher layout. Recently, Hamilton Standard, the originator of the propfan concept, has been paying more attention to a counter-rotating propfan with four or five blades per stage, which eliminates the high-energy swirling wake (recovering some lost power in the process) and alleviates the transmission problem by halving the output torque.

Rolls-Royce has outlined a hybrid engine, the turbofan-prop, in which a small propfan is geared to a conventional cowled fan, which is directly driven by a turbine. Some propulsive efficiency is lost, but swirl effects are reduced and the transmission is very much simplified: it carries less power, at a much more modest ratio. Perhaps the most interesting feature of this proposal, though, is that it can be mounted on an aircraft wing in the same manner as a conventional turbofan engine; it would not need a completely new design of aircraft.

If the propfan is demonstrated successfully in flight, and near-full-scale, in the late 1980s or early 1990s, the way will be open to a production installation on a similar scale. Commercially, the propfan is caught in a cleft stick. Technical risks mean that it will probably not see its first use on a 20–25 000 shp engine for a 150-seater airliner. On the other hand, aircraft below 80 seats or so usually serve very short sectors, where the speed limitations of the conventional propeller are acceptable. A 100-seater, for the mid- to late 1990s (there are now two modern aircraft in that market, the BAe 146 and the Fokker 100) may be the most likely first application in the airline world.

COCKPIT OF THE FUTURE

The airliner cockpit is now half-way through the biggest change in its history. The shape of the next flight deck will depend on the shape of the next new aircraft, but the differences could well be radical. While current technology uses cathode-ray tube (CRT) displays to simulate and improve on the traditional layout, new cockpits will move to different basic concepts, selected for their compatibility with the new technology.

There are two major influences on the future flight deck. One is the continued development of cockpit information systems, using new, larger and more productive CRT or flat-panel displays; the other, of equal impact, is the adoption of electronically signalled controls: fly-by-wire (FBW) and power-by-wire (PBW).

An example of the way the latter might evolve is the development of the first wholly electronic control link in the airline world, the PBW system on the PW2037-powered Boeing 757. The throttle for the new 757 variant was designed within strong commonality constraints, and the linkage is identical above the cockpit floor; the difference is that the control linkage bears on an electronic transducer rather than a pulley. Boeing has also designed a purely electronic throttle to the same requirements. It is much more compact and has no underfloor components. Even so, this would be only an intermediate step to a more refined electronic throttle, which would occupy less space than just the lever and upper pivot of the interim system.

Similarly, the application of FBW to the rudder axis would eliminate the underfloor element of the pedal system. Electrical connections would replace the rudder control, nosewheel steering and brake linkages, and allow the pedal assembly to be moved, to accommodate the pilot's physique, over a much wider range than is now possible.

FBW opens up an almost unlimited range of possibilities in the pitch/roll axis. Mock-ups evaluated by Boeing, for example, include a single, central stick, a conventional wheel, and single or dual vertical sticks mounted on a horizontal 'desk' above the pilot's knees. The last two layouts would provide space for a multi-function keypad controller, similar in nature to the up-front control pad in advanced fighter cockpits but many times more versatile. Techniques have been demonstrated in which the legend on each key can be changed electronically, allowing a simple keypad to perform an enormous number of functions with a single stroke. All these variations could be evaluated thoroughly without the expense of flight testing, thanks to the capability of modern flight simulators.

Whatever the choice of control layout, one of the most important aspects of the FBW and PBW controllers is that they can be designed as modules, because of their small size and the fact that they do not have to be mechanically rigged into the aircraft. This opens up a number of possibilities in flight-deck design. Gradual in-service refinement is possible through the replacement of modules with improved designs. Control modules can be standardised across a manufacturer's entire range of aircraft, as electronic hardware is standardised now.

While future airliners will make use of more advanced electronics and systems, there are no developments on the horizon which will make current production aircraft obsolete by the year 2000. For one thing, as electronics become more advanced, they will also become more compact and easier to install, and it will be no great problem to update the electronic systems in an existing design. Even advanced techniques, such as artificial stability and full-authority fly-by-wire systems, can be exploited without proceeding to a completely new aircraft design; as noted earlier, one way of doing this is to carry fuel in the tail of the aircraft.

So, while the airliners of the year 2000 will incorporate many new technologies, a great many of the aircraft in production are likely to be of very familiar design. There may even be some designs headed for a half-century of continuous production, if the manufacturers' plans hold good.

The largest airliner on the market will probably be a development of the Boeing 747. In the late 1960s, the 747 was designed with considerable potential for 'stretch'; the upper deck could be extended back to the tail, and the fuselage itself could be lengthened by 50 feet without incurring drastic modifications to the rest of the airframe. Development of the aircraft took a different and unexpected tack. Capacity was increased through higher seating densities, while range was maintained and increased by adding fuel capacity and installing steadily more powerful and more efficient engines. By the early 1980s, a new 747 delivered 30 per cent more seat-miles per tonne of fuel than the first prototype, but only a spotter could tell them apart. Only in 1983, however, did the first physically stretched version enter service: the 747-300, with a slightly extended upper deck. The 747 could ultimately go to 700 seats or more, and given the growth rates of the air transport industry this will be plenty in the year 2000.

The idea of twinning aircraft is not new but this Lockheed proposal to join two C-5s is a jumbo an entirely new scale with a capacity up to 1500 passengers

Some time in the late 1980s or early 1990s, the 747 will probably acquire a new wing. A range of 5000 nautical miles, with a full load of passengers and baggage, has become a standard for intercontinental aircraft, and a stretched 747 will need a gross weight in the region of 900 000 lb to achieve it. A modified version of the existing wing would probably suffice, but there are good reasons for Boeing to build a new one. Aerodynamic technology, particularly in the area of transonic sections, has advanced considerably since the 747 was designed, and a new wing could go even further, taking advantage of the immensely powerful aerodynamic simulation computers now under development. Moreover, the 747 wing was designed in the days of cheap fuel, and new aerodynamic knowledge was applied to gain speed rather than to improve fuel consumption.

The new 747 wing would be much bigger, spanning some 250 feet compared with 195 feet for the current wing, more slender in planform and less sharply swept. The lower sweep angle, and the use of aluminium-lithium alloys throughout the structure (this would certainly be possible for an in-service

Left: One of the problems of short haul commuter operations is getting passengers to airports on the peripheries of urban centres in a time which makes the whole operation effective. While helicopters have become urban air taxis to some degree, the prospect of fixed wing V/STOL city-centre operations still looks remote. This Canadair Dash 7 showed off its short landing performance in 1982 by landing in a disused dockyard in London but there is still opposition to overcome before city centre 'STOLports' arrrive

Right: The Franco-Italian ATR 42 is under development as a hopeful contender in the twin turboprop commuter market

date in the early to mid-1990s) would mean that the new wing would weigh little more than the current design. It would probably dispense with low-speed ailerons in favour of electrically signalled spoilers, and might even use some elements of mission-adaptive wing technology, smoothly variable leading-edge flaps for example, to improve low-speed drag and optimise the high-speed section. The new wing might be fitted with winglets, not because it would be more efficient than adding extra span, but because reducing the wingspan would make the aircraft easier to handle on the ground.

The new wing and the more slender fuselage will improve the aerodynamic efficiency of the 747 substantially; this is just as well, since for the reasons explored above there is only a small percentage more to be squeezed out of the powerplant. The 747 will need 60–65 000 lb thrust per engine, and the only way to achieve this without a bigger fan (probably not possible, because of the core/fan-spool mismatching problem) is to drive the fan and its exhaust at a higher speed. Thrust is increased at the expense of propulsive efficiency, and a great deal of development work will be needed just to maintain the engine's cruise fuel consumption. Rolls-Royce sees the turbofan-prop as the only way to break out of this dilemma by the end of the century, at least for larger aircraft.

Until November 1983, there seemed a good chance that the next largest aircraft in production in the year 2000 would be the McDonnell Douglas MD-100, which was to have been a development of the DC-10 incorporating much of the same technology as the new 747 will use. Its abrupt cancellation, combined with the earlier phase-out of the Lockheed TriStar, leaves the 747 as the only long-haul aircraft in production, and it is too large for many routes, particularly the newly developed ones. The intercontinental air transport system, meanwhile, relies for its continuing expansion on improved convenience, and this means increasing the number of city pairs to be served by daily flights.

The trouble is that the market for an airliner designed to serve so-called 'long, thin' routes is small, because such services tend to grow to 747 size within a few years. It is also diminishing because the extended-range versions of the twin-engined wide-body jets can handle many long overland routes. While there may not be enough demand to justify a new aircraft, the long-haul market could be the first to call for 'mid-life updates' on used TriStars and DC-10s. With new engines and aerodynamic refinements, even the medium-range versions of these aircraft have potential for intercontinental range, and they are likely to be replaced by their main operators (the US domestic airlines) in the early 1990s.

LONG HAUL PROPFANS

By the year 2000, though, it is quite possible that a propfan-powered long-haul aircraft could be under development. What makes the small-capacity long-hauler an attractive candidate for propfan power is that its engines are in the 20–25 000 shp category, and could be common to the 100-seat twin which is likely to be the first propfan application. The small long-haul aircraft has an incidental and significant market in military roles, being the right size to be a platform for maritime reconnaissance, airborne warning and control and air refuelling systems.

Medium-range markets in the year 2000 will certainly be dominated by the 'big twins', Boeing's 767, Airbus Industrie's A300/A310, and their derivatives. These types are only starting their development lives. More efficient powerplants, relaxed stability and trim-by-fuel, and the use of aluminium-lithium will be among the major improvements introduced during the 1990s, and stretched 320-seat versions will replace the DC-10 and TriStar in US domestic service. (As noted above, the trijets could well be adapted to long-haul use.) Their extended-range versions will cover a great many long-haul routes.

It remains to be seen whether the restrictions which currently prevent twin-engined aircraft from flying too far from a landing field will be relaxed or removed. Relaxation seems quite likely, particularly in the USA which has a stricter standard than the rest of the world, where it would open up the North Atlantic route to twin-engined aircraft. Removal of the restrictions is possible, in the long term, because dual,

unrelated engine failures are virtually unknown. (Most multiple failures are caused by a common factor, such as fuel starvation.) While the economics of the long-haul twin are attractive, it has some operational disadvantages. Airmanship demands that a twin with a failed or dubious engine has to put down at the nearest airfield, regardless of whether it has even the most rudimentary facilities for maintenance or passenger accommodation. All in all, the industry's built-in conservatism may lead to a preference for multi-engined aircraft on the longer routes.

The development of the 150-seater Airbus A320 will complete the range of new-generation jet airliners, and it will be in production, along with the larger Boeing 757, in the year 2000. The same improvements will be applied to these aircraft as are incorporated on the bigger twins.

The 100-seater bracket is perhaps the most likely to exploit propfan power by the mid- to late 1990s, mainly because the size of the engine is not too daunting. Once again, there are two newly established aircraft already in the market, in the shape of the BAe 146 and Fokker 100, but both could conceivably be fitted with propfans. A propfan powerplant could be fitted to the Fokker 100 without changing more than the rear fuselage, while the high wing of the 146 would make a pylon-mounted installation practical.

Straight wings and subsonic propellers will be the rule for smaller aircraft, where sector lengths are short and the extra speed provided by the propfan is not significant. The propeller, though, is getting more attention than it has received since the 1940s. Composite materials permit the use of new, high-thrust sections; at the same time, composite blades are lighter, reducing loads on the hub. Simpler retention mechanisms make it possible to attach more blades, and six-blade propellers are featured by the British Aerospace ATP and Fokker 50. Both these aircraft are derivatives of 25-year-old designs, fitted with new engines and propellers, aerodynamically and structurally refined and equipped with new and revised systems. They may well be the oldest basic designs still in production in the year 2000; they are large enough to compare reasonably well with new configurations (as noted above, the advantages of such shapes are more pronounced in the smaller size brackets) and their aerodynamics have not been rendered outmoded by the work of the past two decades.

While the 100-seaters may see the first use of propfans, the small commuter airliners may be the first to exhibit radical shapes. Close to the larger business turboprops in size and performance, the 30- to 40-seat commuter aircraft would benefit in many similar ways from advanced configurations, and the lessons learned in developing aircraft such as the Starship and GP-180 will be directly applicable to the design of such an aircraft. A three-surface layout would be particularly suitable, offering high efficiency combined with good airfield performance and very easy loading. The main obstacle to the development of such an aircraft, which is entirely feasible using current technology, is the existence of a number of new aircraft in the market. Competition among these will make the market unreceptive to any newcomer, no matter how good its performance may be, until the early 1990s.

The chances are, then, that an airport apron in the year 2000 will present few unfamiliar spectacles apart from the occasional propfan-powered 100-seater or a canard commuter. But there is a possibility that some new types of aircraft will be in service for specialised transport duties.

COMMERCIAL V/STOL

Stol and Vtol commercial transport has been the subject of a good dozen prototype development programmes and innumerable paper studies over the past few decades, and to say that nobody has made a lot of money out of it is an understatement. Helicopters have established themselves as urban air-taxis, and a sizable industry has developed to support offshore oil and gas rigs, but true public-transport Stol or Vtol operations have been confined to a handful of services worldwide.

Possibly the most promising of Stol concepts is upper-surface blowing (USB) the subject of active investigations in the USA, Japan and the Soviet Union. Most test results to date show that USB can allow a high-subsonic-speed aircraft to operate quite normally from 1500 to 2000 feet of runway, with no cruise penalty and no added subsystems. This is a remarkable achievement, because previous Stol aircraft have always suffered in the cruise (usually from the extra drag of an over-sized wing) or have been mechanically complicated.

USB generates extra lift in two ways: by deflecting the engine exhaust downwards over curved wing flaps, and by 'supercirculation', boosting the airflow over the top of the wing. Because of the extra lift supplied by supercirculation, a USB-configured aircraft can descend rapidly and safely (there is plenty of lift to kill a high sink rate quickly), climb out steeply, or turn sharply while climbing or descending. Thanks to these characteristics, a USB airliner could be used for 'stub-runway' operations at a crowded airport. Demonstrated in service by de Havilland Dash 7s, stub-runway operations involve using Stol aircraft from crosswind runways or taxiways, while larger aircraft use the main runways. The Stol aircraft use separate approach and departure patterns, taking advantage of their manoeuvrability to follow precise tracks well clear of the main traffic. Stub-runway operations can increase the peak traffic flow through an airport by far more

This slew-wing supersonic transport proposal dates from the early '70s when an American SST programme was still very much alive

than the actual volume of Stol operations, because every Stol movement on the stub runway frees a main-runway for a 747.

Perhaps the biggest obstacles in the way of commercial USB are economic. The market for such an aircraft is scattered, and the development costs quite high. Moreover, USB calls for turbofan power, and short-haul markets, where Stol is most valuable, are heading towards the more efficient propeller and propfan. However, the concept may be boosted into production in the Orient. Japan not only has crowded main airports, with noise-conscious neighbours, but also has a great many small airports with wartime 4000-foot runways. Hence the Japanese government's interest in developing a quiet, short-haul airliner with Stol characteristics, for service in the 1990s. A demonstrator aircraft is now flying, and may lead to a production aircraft as Japan's industry continues its long campaign to become a power in world aerospace.

Another Japanese-developed application of USB is the Shinmeiwa Light Amphibian project, a 40-seat amphibious flying-boat intended for transport and other roles in the archipelagos of the East Asian region, where sheltered water is a great deal more abundant than runways. Stol is almost essential for a marine aircraft, reducing lift-off speeds and hence the stresses on the hull; a particular advantage of USB is that it places the engines well out of the spray pattern from the bows. The use of transport seaplanes as a development tool has been receiving some active attention in Singapore, Malaysia and Indonesia, and there is a chance that it could result in a production programme. Otherwise, it seems inevitable that the large marine aircraft will be an extinct species by the end of the century while small amphibians will survive.

Turning to Vtol commercial aircraft, there are probably only two types which stand a chance of carrying fare-paying passengers in the year 2000. One of these is the straightforward helicopter. The commercial uses of helicopters have been limited largely by sheer economics. Helicopters are inefficient in forward flight, and become steadily more so as they get faster, largely because of the drag of the rotor and rotor hub. They are accordingly slow, hence unproductive, and use a great deal of fuel. They are also expensive to maintain.

The way in which some of these attributes are changing is shown by Boeing Vertol's Model 360 demonstrator. Superficially, the Model 360 is a quite conventional tandem-twin-rotor helicopter like Boeing's Chinook, but in detail it is very different. To begin with, it is made almost entirely of composite materials. Even the rotor hubs, final driveshafts and gearbox casings are composite. The aircraft has four-blade rotors, making eight blades in all, and the blades use newly developed sections and profiles.

All these features contribute to a dramatic improvement in conventional helicopter performance, reliability and comfort. Composite materials save weight in the fuselage, but two attributes make them tremendously important to the helicopter: they can be blended and tailored to control stress and vibration, and they are virtually immune to fatigue. Many metal

components in a helicopter must be replaced at regular intervals; composite rotor blades and hubs have vastly increased lives. To reduce vibration, the bane of the helicopter, many dynamic components of the Model 360 are made in 'mixed-modulus' composites. These are special materials in which different fibres, with greater or less elasticity, are blended to provide exactly the right characteristics for a given component. Traditionally, the limitations of metal construction have ruled out major changes in rotor section from root to tip; this has changed now that composites have proven themselves in rotor blades, and designers are now free to tailor the section to the different speeds and loadings encountered by the different parts of the rotor.

The Model 360 rotor is designed for efficient cruise at 205 to 210 mph, within five per cent of the world speed record for a conventional helicopter, set over a short course by a modified Mi-24 'Hind'. The fuselage is clean, and the landing gear is retractable, halving the equivalent flat-plate area of the helicopter compared to a conventional design. The result will be that helicopters using Model 360-type technology will be capable of long-range operations without carrying virtually all their disposable load as fuel. They will be smoother and more appealing to ride, and far cheaper to operate.

The result will be to make the helicopter far more competitive as a commercial transport, possibly allowing it to break into some densely travelled urban corridor routes in Europe or North America. Smaller helicopter-bus services will become more acceptable, and may connect many US airports with their further-flung suburbs. With their point-to-point convenience and direct airport access, helicopters could become a serious rival to the fixed-wing aircraft on shorter commuter flights.

The advanced conventional helicopter could be the biggest rival to the only other Vtol concept on the cards for the year 2000, the Tilt-Rotor. A 40-seat commercial Tilt-Rotor will certainly be technically feasible by then but, equally certainly, it will be a great deal more expensive to buy and maintain than a conventional helicopter. Its great advantage will be its far superior flight performance and cruise efficiency, obtained by eliminating the drag of the rotor.

Tilt-Rotor technology promises to fulfil many of the requirements which earlier commercial Vtols have failed to satisfy. It is nearly as fast as a conventional propeller-driven airliner, and can fly at a comfortable altitude. It takes off without too much noise thanks to the large area of its rotors, and internal noise and vibration seem acceptable. While it is a mechanically complex machine in its present form, the production aircraft will have more advanced and much simpler electronically signalled controls. While its cruise fuel economy will not be as good as that of a conventional airliner, it will not be cripplingly so. Above all, it will be the fastest point-to-point vehicle conceivable, for distances between 100 and 400 miles. Its potential is considerable, and so are the challenges it presents, and its commercial development is going to be interesting.

FUTURE FREIGHTERS

Another specialised type of commercial transport aircraft is the freighter. The development of the air freight industry has always defied accurate long-term prediction. Air freight volume depends not only on the pace of economic expansion, but also on whether the goods which are most produced are themselves suitable candidates for air freight. On top of this, the market for pure freighters is only a part of the air freight business, because a great deal of air freight is carried in the capacious lower holds of wide-body aircraft.

Some of the factors which will cause changes in the air freight business over the next few years are already visible. Higher seating densities on the wide-body airliners, and higher load factors in the cabins, mean more baggage and less revenue freight in the lower holds. Fashionable consumer products tend, more and more, to be imported. They combine high value and low density, and getting them to the market quickly is important, all of which makes the consumer-goods business a strong market for air freight. The market for overnight express-package services has emerged strongly in the USA, and has already led to the creation of some substantial new companies. In time, such services could appear on the international market if postal and customs bureaucracies can be circumvented.

The market for freight aircraft should continue to be robust, but it is overwhelmingly probable that nearly all freight aircraft will continue to be straightforward derivatives of airliners, well into the 1990s. The reasons are economic. Passenger business is on a vastly larger scale than the freight industry, so passenger aircraft are built in far larger numbers than freighters or convertible types, and are accordingly cheaper to acquire and easier to support in service. A commercial version of the C-5B Galaxy would be a spectacularly productive freighter, with outstanding ability to carry outsize or low-density payloads, but the 82nd C-5B (following completion of the USAF order) will unquestionably be a far more expensive aeroplane to build than the 600th 747, will carry an extra burden of certification costs, and the routine air freight traffic will still travel by 747. Possibly, by the late 1990s, a derivative of the McDonnell Douglas C-17 will be developed for the commercial market.

One active sector of the freight market may continue to need unusual equipment: the outsize business. This has been steadily expanding in recent years. Its customers include the energy business, other engineering firms, and, to a growing extent, the aerospace industry itself; as aircraft companies continue to collaborate, spreading the risks and benefits of major new programmes, the long-distance traffic in major airframe components will increase. Helicopter manufacturers, too, have used outsize aircraft to ship completed aircraft over long distances. This, too, could be a market for the C-17 in the later years of the century.

From super-747s to Tilt-Rotors and advanced, three-surface commuterliners, the airlines of the year 2000 will not be starved for choice. The designers will have had time on their hands, and, if the production aircraft of the year 2000 are to be as similar to today's as is now expected, the manufacturers may even begin to make some money. The result: during the 1990s, there will be a fertile climate for new ideas, to form the basis for the next step forward in commercial aviation.

It is not easy to say where that step will be placed. The difficulty of securing further improvements in powerplant efficiency were discussed earlier, but similar considerations may apply to conventional subsonic configurations by the year

2000. Studies of future very advanced commercial aircraft have shown that there is relatively little to be gained from three-axis artificial stability, composite primary structure or increased wing aspect ratio; a few per cent here or there, maybe, but hardly enough to warrant development of a new technology. A few more radical ideas have been the subject of some investigations.

The Philosopher's Stone of subsonic aerodynamics is laminar flow. In a perfect world, a fluid passing over a curved surface, and affected by friction with that surface, will exhibit laminar or 'layered' flow. Velocity close to the surface will be slow, steadily increasing to the free-stream velocity as the distance from the surface increases. The world is not perfect, and laminar flow is a delicate phenomenon. Tiny surface irregularities break up the flow, and it does not re-attach. On a large airliner, the penalty is enormous. Studies have shown that the maintenance of laminar flow over the upper surface of the wing alone could improve the airliner's fuel burn per seat by some 20 per cent.

The problem is achieving that goal, particularly on a large aircraft. Laminar flow is not affected by aircraft size; it is influenced by absolute chord rather than aspect ratio. High-performance sailplanes, which are not very large and have very high aspect ratio, boast astonishing ratios of lift-to-drag approaching fifty to one, well over twice the ratio attained by any large aircraft, because they have tiny wing chord measurements. Their glassfibre wing skins are also very smooth and, in relation to the short chord, very stiff. Achieving natural laminar flow to a significant degree on a large aircraft is generally regarded as impossible.

The alternative is to maintain laminar flow artificially, a technique known as laminar flow control (LFC). This is done by sucking air through pores or slots in the skin, drawing the flow on to the skin, and robbing any eddies of their energy before they can disrupt the main flow. The basic technique was shown to work in the 1960s, but some of the problems identified at that time still remain unsolved. One issue, for example, is the best way to manufacture an LFC wing. A McDonnell Douglas/Nasa test specimen completed in 1982 points to some solutions. The skin is a titanium sheet, perforated with 0·0025-inch diameter holes by an electron beam. There are 1600 holes to each square inch of the surface. The skin is bonded to a corrugated composite panel which acts as a substructure and provides integral air ducts in the corrugations. The skins would be welded together to form wing panels, to eliminate the discontinuities caused by mechanical fasteners.

The LFC wing is highly sensitive to any surface irregularity, and even a squashed insect will break down the flow. The McDonnell Douglas/Nasa test section incorporates a combined leading-edge flap and shield, which protects the wing until the aircraft is out of the insect world's operating regime, and a fluid decontamination system. This is also expected to alleviate the problem of clogged LFC pores.

One of the fundamental problems with LFC is the question of size. Because it is not a 'scaleable' phenomenon, laminar flow cannot be accurately predicted from subscale tests. Developing the technology for a large LFC airframe will call for technology demonstration on a similar scale (perhaps a used wide-body airframe could be fitted with an LFC wing) to establish confidence in the principle.

Some radical configurations offering payload improvements for large aircraft have been identified. The question is whether they will be acceptable to the airline industry, even in the early 2000s. Some of them are designed to spread a greater proportion of the aircraft's weight evenly along the span, reducing the stresses on the wing. The flying-wing 'spanloader' is the ultimate conclusion of such efforts, but it is hard to see how it could be adapted to carry passengers with any degree of efficiency. Multibody configurations are another way of approaching the same problem; once again, they involve questions of operability and accommodation which have not yet been addressed.

There is one approach, though, which offers a quantum jump forward in air travel and potentially competitive economics. It uses technology which is clearly identified and is now the subject of very well funded research and development programmes. The airliner world has virtually ignored it for the last half-decade, but it is almost the only road open to a medium-term improvement in air vehicle efficiency. Given the directions in which technology has been developing over the past few years, it is time to take another look at a supersonic transport (SST) for the year 2000. SSTs can combine the aerodynamic efficiency of LFC with the propulsive efficiency of the propfan, without the mechanical complexity of either. For a good number of reasons, they may never be as economical as subsonic aircraft; but on the other hand, they do a much better job of transporting people.

The aerodynamic efficiency of the SST stems from the fact that an aircraft expends most of its energy supporting its weight. If it can do the same job while supporting its weight for a shorter time, it will use less energy. This concept is expressed in the Mach × lift/drag (M × L/D) formula, which provides a rule-of-thumb comparision of efficiency for aircraft of different speeds. A typical subsonic has a lift/drag ratio of about 16, and cruises at Mach 0·8; an advanced SST would have an L/D of at least 10 and a Mach 2 cruise speed. Comparative M × L/D would be 12·8 for the subsonic, and 20 for the SST, an improvement of over 50 per cent.

Engine efficiency stems from the fact that the gas turbine cycle is highly suited to the supersonic performance regime. The exhaust velocity of a simple very-low-bypass jet engine provides excellent propulsive efficiency for a Mach 2 aircraft, and there is no need for mechanically complicated additions such as fans or advanced propellers. At supersonic speed, a specific fuel consumption (SFC) of 1·3-1·4 lb/hr is entirely feasible; while subsonic engines have much better SFC, the SST engine is covering the ground two and a half to three times faster, so its consumption per mile is much better.

What has made the SST unattractive and inefficient is weight. SST structures soak at high temperatures, reducing permissible stress levels for the materials in the airframe. SSTs must be much more rigid than subsonic aircraft, because of high-speed flutter considerations, and SST cabins operate at a higher pressurisation differential because of the high altitudes at which they fly. The result is that the empty weight per seat of a Concorde is more than three times that of a 747.

Developing technology, however, seems to be closing the gap between the subsonic and the SST. Supersonic-cruise configurations, notably the cranked-arrow wing, are showing

This advanced 200-seat SST proposal from Lockheed might have the range to avoid overflying populated areas and a payload able to achieve truly economic supersonic commercial operations

much greater efficiency improvements than have been forthcoming in the subsonic regime. Supersonic propulsion is also seeing great improvements as a result of the USAF's new fighter engine programme.

Structure weight on a future SST could be reduced by applying the improved stiffness characteristics of modern materials such as aluminium-lithium alloys and advanced composites, possibly of the metal-matrix type. As noted earlier, structures designed for stiffness, such as an SST airframe, derive greater weight benefits from such technology than conventional airliner airframes ever can.

An advanced arrow wing planform could be integrated into a three-surface layout. Both the choice of planform and the elimination of trim drag would serve to reduce the size and weight of the wing compared with a Concorde-type configuration. Full-authority fly-by-wire would present no problems; the advanced SST would also use electronic/aerodynamic structural mode control, as applied to the B-1 bomber, as a substitute for physical stiffness. Bending and flexing moments would be sensed electronically and countered by control forces in the foreplane and tail. Mission-adaptive wing technology could be used to reduce spanwise bending loads, either reducing weight or allowing a higher aspect ratio in a thin-section supersonic wing. The latter would be desirable, improving performance at lower speeds and, once again, allowing the overall size of the wing to be reduced.

One of the bigger design challenges would be the creation of an acceptably quiet engine. Probably, in the interests of reduced noise, some degree of variable bypass would have to be introduced into the basically simple engine. A number of concepts have been tested for the variable cycle engine (VCE); all of them, however, are low-bypass jet engines in which the core and bypass flows can be regulated independently through systems of variable stators and movable valves. Some of the designs studied take advantage of a rather surprising phenomenon. While turbofan engines naturally exhaust their high-speed core stream inside the low-speed fan stream, it has been found that inverting this velocity profile, so that the high-speed flow is on the outside, markedly reduces the engine's noise level. One proposed SST engine from Pratt & Whitney even has burners in the fan duct, which are, paradoxically enough, ignited to reduce noise at low speeds. The weight penalty of the features added to the engine and nacelle to reduce noise would be substantial, but could be reduced by the extensive use of advanced materials, and the powerplant weight would be reduced overall by the use of a short, high-stage-loading core similar to those being developed for the Joint Advanced Fighter Engine.

The key to SST productivity will be a vast payload-range improvement over the Concorde; the key to its economics and its environmental acceptability will be providing that performance within a reasonable gross weight.

The advanced SST would be a 200-seater, simply because a smaller aeroplane would be economically restricted to an unrealistically small slice of the travel market. It would have a similar Mach 2 cruising speed to the Concorde (above Mach 2, heating considerations begin to dominate the entire design). Range would be much greater than that of the Concorde. Ideally, an advanced SST would have sufficient range to tackle nearly all of today's non-stop sectors while detouring around densely populated areas. It would be feasible, and very desirable, to design it with the ability to cruise at Mach 1·15 for part of its flight without sacrificing range; on a flight from London to Los Angeles, for example, it could cross the Atlantic and the north of Canada at supersonic speed, and continue across the United States almost 50 per cent faster than a subsonic, without leaving a 'boom' on the ground. (Mach 1·15 at 40 000 feet is less than the speed of sound at sea level.)

The advanced SST would have to be reasonably quiet, although it would not have to match the quietest aircraft; supersonics will never form a large percentage of airport movements. It would have to be reasonably fuel-efficient, but this is less crucial than one might think. Because the supersonic aircraft would carry only the high-fare business passengers, its fuel costs might well be a much smaller percentage of revenues than they would be in the case of a 747 full of holidaymakers. Both these standards imply that the range and payload minima should be met within a gross weight of 600-650 000 lb.

The management and marketing of the programme will have to be as innovative as the aircraft if it is to make any commercial sense. Almost certainly, it will be too big to be handled by private industry alone, and governments will have to become involved. Leasing the aircraft might be easier than selling them, because they will, inevitably, be expensive; not only will the research and development cost be high, but the aircraft will be so productive that comparatively few of them will satisfy a large share of the business travel market. Also, making the aircraft available for lease on equal terms to all qualified operators might head off an attempt by non-supersonic airlines to fix astronomically high fare levels for supersonic flights.

0.7

Personal Aircraft

Rutan Grizzley, a bold new shape in the sky

Of all the tasks which aircraft undertake, none involves as many aircraft of as many different types as personal transport. From the smallest microlight to the Saudi Government's $130 million 747-300, a common thread links them all, they are assigned to take a specific person or group of people where they want to go, when they want to go, under their own control. All of them, whether owned by private citizens, corporations or governments, can be described as 'personal aircraft'.

The personal aircraft of the year 2000 will come in a still greater variety of shapes and sizes. Development over the next few years will follow two very different tracks. Today's purpose-built personal jets are already highly advanced aircraft, with airframes, engines and equipment close to the standards set by new-generation airliners. Their development will be largely evolutionary, with a few substantial changes possible by the end of the century. Some of the trends in that sector will be outlined later. Among smaller aircraft, encompassing most of the propeller-driven types, the picture is very different, and long overdue changes are to be expected.

Dominated for many years by three major companies based in the midwestern USA, the business of building smaller aircraft for personal transport has gained a reputation for ultra-conservatism. Personal aircraft have tended to be decades old in design, and development work has often been confined to a new paint scheme every year. Times have started to change, to such an extent that new personal aircraft are leading some areas of technology. Developments at opposite ends of the spectrum will spread to the entire market by the mid-1990s.

Traditional light planes and small business aircraft were well suited to the post-1945 structure of the industry, which used war-surplus plants and a vast pool of trained labour to build affordable, rugged light aircraft. They set no records for aerodynamic efficiency, but fuel was cheap. As fuel prices and labour costs outran the general rate of inflation in the 1970s, though, conventional aircraft became steadily more expensive to buy and operate. The growth of the industry slowed, and by the early 1980s the manufacturers were in serious trouble.

From the vantage point of the 1990s, three developments of the 1970s will be seen as milestones in the reshaping of the smaller personal aircraft. None of them was initially recognised as such and at least one was regarded as a lunatic aberration.

The last-mentioned was the sport of hang-gliding. Paradoxically, the innovation which made the new sport feasible was a spin-off from the space programmes of the 1960s: the Rogallo wing, a braced, flexible delta wing which had originally been designed to recover rocket boosters. Work on the Rogallo as a steerable parachute inspired a few reckless souls to start leaping off cliffs and steep hills, attached to their gliders by straps and harnesses.

ENTER THE MICROLIGHT

Trudging back up the hill to the launching point, hang-glider pilots naturally began to think of installing engines and propellers on their flying machines. Early efforts were directed towards powered Rogallos, but the layout was not very suited to powered flight. Its legacy to aviation, as the early powered hang-gliders gave way to more conventional 'microlight' aircraft, was the rediscovery of light, cheap aerostructures, consisting of flexible skins in tension, a minimal rigid skeleton and bracing wires. Abandoned since the earliest days of flying, and now combined with advanced light alloys and new synthetic fabrics, these techniques have created aircraft which are light, simple, cheap and portable, while being quite airworthy. Their importance is that they make flying affordable again, for the sort of people who have been priced out of flying in conventional light aircraft.

The second milestone of the 1970s was the appearance of Burt Rutan's VariEze homebuilt aircraft. Tremendously innovative, the VariEze was the first canard aircraft to see large-scale use, and the first powered aircraft made of composite materials to be built in any numbers. Key features of the design include the integration of a small canard, winglets and leading-edge root extensions in a configuration which overcomes or offsets many of the traditional disadvantages of a

Burt Rutan's VariEze home-built aircraft of the 1970s pioneered many of the shapes and concepts now showing up in much larger business aircraft such as canards, winglets, composite construction and leading edge root extensions The Rutan Quickie (left) homebuilt incorporated canard foreplanes with the landing gear while the VariViggen (Right foreground) and VariEze (background) have been built in large numbers by home constructors in many countries

tail-first layout.

A third significant event was the launch of the Learfan 2100 business aircraft in late 1979. The last design of Bill Lear, the creator of the Learjet, the Learfan was the first propeller-driven light aircraft in decades to present any technical novelty worth mentioning. As these words are written, the Learfan is expected to be certificated in 1984 as the world's first aircraft to be built primarily of advanced composite materials.

While the Learfan is not a canard design, it has a unique high-efficiency configuration. The engines are buried in the rear fuselage, unusable empty space on a conventional light aircraft, and drive a single propeller through extension shafts and a coupling gearbox.

The microlight, the VariEze and the Learfan are the pointers to the personal aircraft of 2000. By that time, there will be few aircraft in production that do not owe something, directly or indirectly, to the pioneering developments of the 1970s. The first signs of this trend are now clearly visible, having emerged strongly in the course of 1983.

Signs are visible at all levels in the market. The Eipper company, one of the reputable manufacturers of microlight aircraft, has hired Burt Rutan to design and develop a new aircraft. It will be factory-built and no more expensive than a sports car, an appropriate analogy because its engine will be built by Britain's Lotus Cars. Unlike previous microlights, it will be a clean, sleek design in the VariEze style.

Direct Rutan influence is also apparent in the Beech Starship 1, unveiled in October 1983 and typifying the coming changes at the top end of the market. Resembling a giant VariEze, the Starship is reported to stem from Rutan's unbuilt Defiant 2 design, and his Scaled Composites company built the seven-tenths-scale proof-of-concept vehicle flown in August 1983. Unveiled at the same time as the Starship was the US-Italian Gates-Piaggio GP-180, of comparable performance but using a three-surface aerodynamic layout. Also revealed in 1983 was the Avtek 400, of smaller size and comparable performance.

All the developments are indicators of coming change. Direct replacements for the propeller-driven personal aircraft

The OMAC 1, so far the only advanced-technology design for a single engined business aircraft pressurised for flight at heights above and out of the weather

of today may have very different shapes, be built of completely different materials and have radically different engines. In addition, there may be new types of aircraft on the market which do not correspond directly to anything available today. The entire structure of the industry is beginning to adapt to new conditions. Reflecting the move towards high technology, Beech has been taken over by the electronics-based Raytheon group. Cessna is to develop new light-aircraft technology in collaboration with defence giant General Dynamics, while the third 'big three' company, Piper, was acquired by avionics, industrial and military combine Lear Siegler in late 1983.

WHITHER THE BIZJET?

While the propeller-driven types now in production will be replaced by new and radically different designs, exactly what shape these will take is another question. It is likely that there will be more diversity than exists today. The flightline of a typical business-and-private airport could present an interesting spectacle: Rutan-type canards, various types of tandem-wing aircraft, three-surface configurations, Learfan-type pushers and the rest. Particularly among the smaller aircraft, though, the traditional front-engine, rear-tail configuration will survive, for the same reason that front-engine, rear-drive cars have survived: there is such a large body of knowledge about their handling characteristics that they will continue to set standards for natural flying behaviour.

Twin-engined aircraft are perhaps the most likely to change, because of the attractions of moving more of the thrust towards the centreline. The ultimate in such arrangements is the Learfan, in which both engines drive a single propeller. While this arrangement may seem mechanically complex, with its long driveshafts and coupling gearbox, it is no more so than a helicopter transmission; the main obstacle to its wider adoption may be the comparable attractiveness of direct-drive, twin-propeller pusher layouts such as those of the Avtek, GP-180 and Starship. By locating the engines and pusher propellers above the rear-mounted wing of a canard, the designers of the latter aircraft have been able to use higher-speed, smaller-diameter propellers located, because there is no longer a problem with cabin noise, close alongside a narrow, tapered rear fuselage, and have greatly reduced the asymmetric-power problem without introducing a new element into the propulsion system.

While these twin-propeller canard configurations share few common points with the Learfan at first sight, all of them are aimed at overcoming the same basic deficiencies of the conventional 'on-the-wing' twin-engine design. One of the main reasons for the coming radical change in the shape of the light aircraft, in fact, is that the traditional layout is so far from optimum. Design problems have increased with the development of faster, higher-powered twins. Larger engines need bigger propellers, so the engines have to be moved further outboard. In the most critical one-engine-inoperative (OEI) case, where one engine fails just at the moment of take-off, powerful asymmetric forces are generated, and the aircraft must have large and effective control surfaces to cope with them. This means either a long tail (which is too far from the centre of gravity to accommodate any useful load) or large, heavy and drag-producing tail surfaces. Even so, it is impractical to provide more than the bare minimum of OEI performance in a light twin. A conventional layout also places the noise of engines and propellers close to the cabin.

Above: The Lear Fan Prototype's pusher layout required a rapid means of divesting the propeller in an emergency

Right: The Lear Fan uses two turboshafts coupled by extension shafts and a combining/reduction gearbox with separate clutches to drive a single propeller. The propeller itself is made of Kevlar composite with stainless steel leading edges

While most heavy commercial aircraft use the conventional on-the-wing layout, bigger aircraft can cope more easily with its disadvantages. For example, their larger cabins can be made longer in relation to their width, so that there is less unused tail volume. Jets are a special case, too, because the engines can be slung well ahead of the wing, and the rear fuselage made longer again. Because of the special problems faced by smaller aircraft, they will be the first to adopt new configurations.

All four of the new high-technology business aircraft under development in 1983 fall into a similar category: twin-turboprop aircraft with cruising speeds around 400 mph, or about Mach 0·6, and service ceilings in the region of 40 000 feet. There is a good reason for this similarity in performance. The new aircraft do not compete directly with most current conventional aircraft, but fall into a distinct market niche of their own. They are slower than most jet or turbofan aircraft, but much faster and somewhat more expensive than most conventional turboprops. This has helped them get started in the market, but it will be only a matter of time before their technology spreads to other types.

EFFICIENT CRUISE

Each aerodynamic layout has its own advantages. Beech is likely to extend the use of the Rutan-type configuration, characterised by a rear-mounted, sweptback wing and small foreplan at the extreme nose. It offers a clean and efficient cruise configuration, and a long fuselage length uninterrupted by wing structure. The main wing, however, is too far aft to carry the fuel load or to be fitted with powerful flaps (the Starship's are notably small). The wing has to be made larger to compensate, and the fuel has to be located in the deep wing-root extensions. Both of these features imply a certain weight and drag penalty, as does the wing sweep needed for stability.

The three-surface layout used on the GP-180 is, by contrast, intended to optimise the performance of the wing. The use of the canard for nose-up trim reduces the load on the wing, because the trim force adds to the total lift. Together with the large flaps made possible by a three-surface layout, this means that the GP-180 can get by with a wing no larger than that of a Cessna 172. Minimal wing area is particularly useful for a high-performance aircraft, which has plenty of power available for take-off and other low-speed cases such as a go-around following an abandoned landing, and which does not need a large wing to meet cruise performance targets. On the debit side, the three-surface layout is more complex than the Rutan configuration, and does not yield quite as much uninterrupted cabin length.

The Avtek 400's configuration is different again, with only a short horizontal distance between the front and rear wings. The key to its stability is the vertical separation between the high-mounted front wing and the low-set rear surface. While the Avtek 400 had not flown in late 1983, it was expected to offer good cruise efficiency, and has compactness and simplicity on its side; both these attributes tend to make its configuration applicable to smaller aircraft.

There may be other variations on the configuration theme. The remarkable tandem-winged Quickie, bearing some resemblance to the Avtek with its equal-sized wings, has already been developed into the improved two-seaters Q2 and Q200, and could be the forerunner of new and much more efficient factory-built light aircraft. One variation on the tandem-wing theme which has been the subject of some studies is the rhomboidal planform, in which the sweptback front wing and the sweptforward rear wing are connected at the tips for extreme structural efficiency. As yet, though, such radical and peculiar-looking layouts have not formed the basis of any firm design studies.

Under the skin, the personal aircraft of the year 2000 will be equally radical. The switch to composite materials in the world of light aircraft will be faster and more complete than in

the heavy military or civil business, for a number of good reasons. Light aircraft present a relatively undemanding structural environment, with lower peak stresses and less critical stiffness requirements than are encountered in a high-performance fighter or a large airliner, and this makes it possible to use nearly all the very large range of composite materials, including glasses and synthetics such as Kevlar, with very few restrictions. Many of these materials are much less costly than the carbon composites needed for fighters or airliners.

Small aircraft are produced at high rates, and low construction cost can be a crucial marketing advantage. Some of the construction techniques now in sight for composites offer tremendous reductions in the numbers of workhours going into a light aircraft. The use of composites can eliminate many fasteners in favour of 'co-curing' where separate subcomponents are fused into one assembly during manufacture. Factory-built aircraft may also use versions of the technique developed for sailplanes and the VariEze, where the composite skin is kept in shape not by complex assemblies of ribs and stringers but by rigid plastic foam cores. This eliminates a vast number of parts, and is more suitable for light aircraft, where internal volume is not critical, than for military aircraft or airliners.

The fact that light aircraft are small is another factor in favour of the rapid expansion of composite manufacture. Many of the cost and structural benefits of composites are best realised by designing one-piece, continuous components, and in a small aircraft this is possible without unduly large or complex tooling.

Power for these new aircraft will come from a variety of sources. One thing is certain, present market conditions, where two turbine engines and two very similar ranges of piston engines have dominated the market for propeller-driven aircraft, will be challenged. Like the airframe scene, the engine market has been dominated by conversatism, and there have been few significant technical innovations in light-aircraft powerplants since the early 1960s, when the first successful turbine engines were introduced. The technical scene at the moment is very fluid, and no strong competition to the established order has emerged as yet. Some of the candidates, though, are worthy of note.

The Rutan Defiant proof-of-concept prototype first flew in 1978 with a push-pull twin engine and canard layout

The turboprop will probably dominate the higher market brackets. Its light weight, its ability to provide high power smoothly and with reasonable efficiency, and its compatibility with aircraft performance characteristics in that its power falls off with altitude, more or less in line with the total drag of the aircraft, make it well suited to a high-altitude, high-cruising-speed aircraft.

The small gas turbine, though, has two related drawbacks when compared to an intermittent-combustion (IC) engine, a term which covers both reciprocating piston engines and Wankel-type rotaries. One problem is that it has a lower pressure ratio, and therefore tends to be less fuel-efficient than the IC engine. The other disadvantage is that it costs more to build, to buy and to maintain. The two drawbacks are related, for the simple reason that almost anything that is done to improve the efficiency of the turbine to IC levels tends to drive up its costs, in research and development, maintenance and manufacture.

Small gas turbines have specific problems of their own, not fully shared by their larger relations. For instance, the efficiency of a turbine stage is limited by the effects of the boundary layer around the drum, at the blade root, and by the leakage of air around its tip. Other things being equal, the boundary layer is no less thick on a small drum than on a large one, and clearances between the blade tip and the engine case are not necessarily smaller on a small engine. Further physical barriers include the difficulty of building an efficient air-cooling system into a tiny turbine blade, and the inefficiencies and flow distortions caused by surface roughness.

Comparisons between turbine and IC performance are academic in most aerospace applications, where the sheer power or speed requirements rule out IC engines. Not so with a small, propeller-driven aircraft; there is going to be an interesting battle in the 500-800 shp band over the next few years. Above 800 shp, the issue is likely to be decided by outside factors. There is really no serious competition between turbine and IC for helicopter applications, because weight is so critical, and the US Army is pumping a great deal of money into a new and advanced small turbine for its LHX advanced scout helicopter. This up-front investment will probably result in a two-company, full-scale demonstration programme, and it is a safe bet that both participants will develop civil turbines from their LHX powerplants. These will incorporate features such as cheap and durable ceramic components, advanced electronic control systems and controlled-diffusion aerodynamics, and will have reasonable fuel consumption and moderate maintenance costs. The headway gained by their military backing will probably eliminate any serious competition.

SUPERCHARGING AND DIESELS

In lower power brackets, though, small-turbine problems rapidly become more acute, and advanced IC technology becomes more attractive. The key is supercharging. While this has been a feature of small aircraft piston engines for many years, it has not been taken anywhere near its limits on current light-aircraft powerplants. Instead, supercharging has been applied to minimally modified unsupercharged engines, to improve high-altitude performance. Only recently has a light-aircraft powerplant been fitted with an aftercooler, which lowers the temperature but not the pressure of the air leaving the supercharger and allows higher boost pressures without detonation. Highly turbocharged IC engines, on the other hand, can attain extremely high overall pressure ratios, leading to competitive power/weight figures and very low specific fuel consumption, within the bounds of known technology.

Two attractive candidates for future development are the Wankel-type rotary engine and the two-stroke, very-high-compression diesel. The rotary offers light weight, smoothness and low frontal area, comparable to that of a turbine, while the diesel has even better fuel consumption and, surprisingly, lower weight. While diesels are not usually associated with light weight, the highly turbocharged two-stroke can generate so much power from each cubic inch of swept volume that the heavily built reciprocating components are relatively small. The pressures and temperatures encountered would probably be beyond the capability of air-cooled engines, and the liquid-cooled engine is likely to make a comeback.

Electronic systems would be used to control such power-

The US-Italian Gates-Piaggio GP 180's three surface, pusher-propeller layout brings a payoff in reduced cabin noise

plants. While turbines have long held a monopoly on simple control mechanisms, the availability of powerful, rugged and affordable electronic controls will bring 'single-lever' control to highly supercharged IC engines. A single control will regulate propeller pitch, fuel injection, boost pressure, cooling and, in non-diesel engines, ignition.

Power will be delivered, in most cases, through conventional propellers. Some top-line aircraft may graduate to propfan power (discussed more fully in Chapter 6) but most propeller-driven personal aircraft operate on such short sectors that the extra speed made possible by the propfan cannot really be exploited to offset its greater costs. The standard propeller will continue to improve and evolve. The special characteristics of composite materials, in particular their extreme stiffness, and the fact that they can be tailored to provide maximum stiffness in any given direction, have lifted many of the traditional design restrictions on propellers. For example, it is now possible to design propeller blades which have both high-speed aerofoil sections and efficient, high-aspect-ratio planforms, two characteristics which used to be mutually exclusive. Because composite blades are lighter, they need less bulky restraining mechanisms at the hub, and it becomes possible to design light and practical hubs with six or more blades. The small-diameter, six-blade propeller will find a niche in the market between the more conventional propeller and the propfan.

In the cockpit of the small personal aircraft, new technology may be applied to a greater extent than many people might expect. Based on mass-produced CRTs and standardised electronic components, tv-type flight instruments may oust conventional gauges from even the cheapest aircraft. Medium-priced aircraft such as high-performance single-engine types could acquire more sophisticated systems to make in-weather flying easier and safer.

Another likely change in the market for smaller personal aircraft is the emergence of some new categories. The Eipper-Lotus project, and France's Robin ATL, foreshadow the appearance of new aircraft falling clearly between the microlights and the smallest current factory-built types. Slow-flying, slow-landing, cheap and efficient, these may well be powered by converted car engines to reduce costs. Unlike the true microlights, they will have room for two in an enclosed cabin. Like microlights, though, they will be easily transportable. Property prices have boosted hangarage to a painfully high proportion of operating costs, but few light aircraft since the Moth of the 1930s have been designed to be towed behind a car and kept in a garage. By the year 2000, such aircraft could be the standard basic trainers for private pilots, helping the transition of unlicenced microlight pilots to more advanced aircraft.

OUT OF THE WEATHER

The range of types on the market will also be joined by the high-performance single-engined aircraft, pressurised for flight above the weather and with considerable power and range. Cessna's P210 was alone in the pressurised-single category for many years; it has now been joined by the Mooney 301, and Beech is working on the turboprop-powered Lightning. So far, the only advanced-technology design in this

Truly personal aircraft have long been an aviation dream. In the US in the '30s and '40s there was a flurry of 'roadables', aircraft that turned into cars and in the 1950s a plethora of lifting platforms and jet packs that did little to impress the US Army, nor turn commuting into a matter of hovering to work. Personal aircraft of the year 2000 are still likely to be for recreation only and this 1930s dream of the businessman of the future in his twin rotor helicopter remain unrealised

category is the OMAC 1 canard prototype, but there is clearly a great deal of scope for configuration and powerplant innovations. In fact, these 'super-singles' present some interesting design challenges. They are probably close to the ultimate in aircraft which are to be flown by their owners, so they must be designed for safe operation by a single part-time pilot, year-round in all weathers. This will drive future advanced designs in two directions. A high cruising altitude above 35 000 feet will mean that the aircraft can fly above most of the weather, while good climb performance will mean that the aircraft can pass quickly through bad weather as its climbs to altitude. The second distinctive aspect of these aircraft will be the use of advanced electronics to reduce the pilot's workload. Microprocessors and clear, graphic CRT displays will help the pilot control communications and navigation functions; electronics will simplify engine control and monitor the other aircraft systems. The elimination of prolonged 'in-weather' flying, and the use of advanced control systems, should actually make these high-performance aircraft safer for the part-time pilot than today's lower-flying aircraft.

Higher-powered single-engined aircraft could fill many roles now served by the smaller twins. Single-engined aircraft are inherently cheaper to buy and maintain, and are more reliable than twins. Among smaller aircraft, too, there seems to be little significant difference in safety between singles and twins. This market shift will have an effect on the powerplant business, creating a need for affordable and efficient engines in the 400-700 shp bracket.

Business jets, as noted earlier, will probably not see such sweeping changes in the same timescale. Corporate jets, which started life in the early 1960s as fighters with cabins, have become steadily more refined and fully equipped. Inertial navigation systems, digital avionics and CRT flight instruments have been adopted enthusiastically, and their use has spread more quickly through business jets than large commercial aircraft. But the corollary of this improvement in standards is that a brand-new corporate jet is now very expensive to develop and put into production, just like a new airliner. Development costs have to be passed on to the customer, in the form of higher prices, and because corporate aircraft do nothing like as much flying as airliners in the course of a year, their purchase price is a very important part of the hourly operating cost. It is much cheaper to do what Gulf-

stream Aerospace has done with the Gulfstream III and IV, and progressively incorporate new technology into the existing airframe. The Gulfstream IV even carries the same philosophy into its Rolls-Royce Tay engines, derivatives of the 1960s-technology Spey engine incorporating features of the company's latest civil powerplants.

Some of today's business jets, therefore, are very likely to remain in production and service by the year 2000, although continuous modification will have made virtually new aircraft out of them. But there are some factors which may lead to further innovations by the later 1990s.

One of these will be market pressure from new aircraft powered by advanced turboprops, which will offer many of the jet's traditional advantages such as near-jet speed, high cruising altitude and low internal noise, combined with much lower fuel consumption and competitive prices. Advanced turboprops will probably eliminate smaller, slower jets from the market, and could drive the surviving small jets in the direction of higher speed, where jets hold an advantage, and greater range to take advantage of speed in lower trip times.

Some of the smaller jets are already appearing in higher-powered, faster versions, taking advantage of new engine and aerodynamic technology. In the longer term, new, very efficient small jets capable of high subsonic speeds could enter the market. The forward-swept wing, now under test on the Grumman X-29, might be a very attractive layout for such aircraft. Using composite skins and the well understood technology of aeroelastic tailoring, a sweptforward wing can be lighter and more efficient than a sweptback wing for a comparable Mach number, and has naturally good low-speed handling. Its great advantage for a small business aircraft, though, is that it makes for a very tidy, compact configuration. Sweptback wings have to pass beneath the cabin floor, giving the conventional small jet an unsightly and inefficient ventral bulge; deep supercritical sections have worsened this problem. A sweptforward wing, however, can pass neatly through the fuselage behind the cabin, at the optimum mid position.

BABY-JETS

Another potential new class of aircraft, also with the emphasis on performance, is the 'baby jet', a small and relatively cheap aircraft designed to put jet speed and jet prestige in the hands of the owner-pilot. Gulfstream Aerospace's Peregrine may be a forerunner of this class, also represented by the British Chichester-Miles Leopard project. While there is an element of the ultimate plaything about some of these aircraft, they certainly have some potential. Jet engines are basically the simplest of powerplants, and advanced instruments and navigation systems should put a simple jet well within the competence of a part-time pilot. The development of the cruise missile has spawned a generation of small turbofan engines, making it possible to design such aircraft for low noise and reasonable fuel efficiency. While the small jet will be less efficient than the advanced single-turboprop types discussed earlier in the chapter, it is potentially much faster; it could become as much of a fashion in the 1990s as was the original Learjet 23 in the 1960s.

A less probable, but still possible development is the supersonic corporate transport. Its emergence would be intimately linked to that of a new supersonic airliner; it would use very similar technology, albeit on a smaller scale, and demand for it would arise as corporate users became accustomed to supersonic speeds, just as the introduction of the 707 and DC-8 spurred development of the first corporate jets.

At the opposite end of the speed scale will be vertical-take-off personal aircraft. It is a safe prediction than nearly all of these will be straightforward helicopters. There is one possible exception. If the US joint-service Tilt-Rotor programme proceeds on the schedule currently planned, a smaller commercial version might see service by the late 1990s. It may prove attractive to some companies, such as oil-industry giants, with particularly intractable transport problems, but such a development would not cloud the prospects for the conventional helicopter.

Composites have already made helicopters more efficient, more reliable and cheaper to maintain, and they will continue to do so. The first helicopters to be designed primarily for personal transport are now demonstrating their usefulness in many roles, particularly for organisations which need to be located in traffic-bound urban areas.

The next generation of personal helicopters will feature all-composite airframes and rotor systems, and composites will also be used in many parts of the transmission. New rotor sections, made possible by composite technology, will lift normal operating speeds towards the 200 mph mark, without a disproportionate increase in drag, and range and efficiency will be improved accordingly. Future helicopters will also be smoother and quieter internally, and advanced electronics will make them easier to fly, particularly in poor weather. Current helicopters can already beat business jets on some short trips, by dodging the traffic between city centre and airport; the faster the helicopter, the greater the distance over which it can sustain this advantage. Smaller helicopters will also be more widely accepted for personal use, as they become faster, smoother and, a very important consideration for an urban vehicle, quieter.

In the year 2000, though, the majority of personal aircraft will be flown for plain fun. The homebuilding fraternity will be as active as ever and, given the degree to which they have broken the trail for the newest aircraft from the big manufacturers, one can only wonder what strange and hyper-efficient shapes they will be putting into the sky.

While 'super-microlights' will be big business, the merits of the current microlight will continue to endear it to the hardy. Like the pioneer aircraft of the early 1900s, which in many respects they resemble, they can be stored in a small space, easily transported and flown from a small open field. Microlights and their advanced developments could put flying back within the reach of anyone of ample enthusiasm and moderate means, and in the process could do aviation a greater service than almost any other type of aircraft.

It is refreshing to conclude this chapter, and this book, with one quite impractical, just-for-fun type of aircraft. This is also one case where development up to the year 2000 can be predicted with almost complete confidence. The type in question is the hot-air balloon. Now thriving into its third century with no significant changes, it seems unlikely to need any in the next decade and a half.

INDEX

S

T

U

V

W

X, Y

Picture credits:

Front Cover: Gates Learjet, Pages 2–3: McDonnell Douglas, 8–9: National Air and Space Museum, 11: Rolls-Royce, 12: Flight, 13: Beechcraft, 14 (top): Gates Learjet, 14 (below): Avtek, 15: McDonnell Douglas, 16: NASA, 18–19: General Dynamics, 19: NASA, 20: Boeing, 21: NASA, 22: Hughes Helicopters, 23: NASA, 24: US Department of Defense (DoD), 25 (top): Lockheed, 25 (below): Sikorsky, 26: British Aerospace, 27: British Aerospace, 29: General Electric, 31: USAF, 34: McDonnell Douglas, 35: McDonnell Douglas, 36: British Aerospace (via Flight), 36: Plessey, 37: USAF, 38: USAF, 39: Grumman, 40: Grumman, 41: Dassault-Breguet, 42: Thomson-CSF, 42 (right): Airbus Industrie, 43: Rediffusion, 44: Canadair, 45: Boeing, 47: NASA, 48: Lockheed, 50–51: NASA, 54 (main picture): McDonnell Douglas, 55: USAF, 56: USAF, 57: DoD, 58–59: NASA, 61: Rockwell, 63: Grumman, 64: General Dynamics, 65 (top): USAF, 65 (below): Lockheed, 66–67: USAF, 69: Grumman, 70–71: USAF, 72: Dassault Breguet, 73 (top): McDonnell Douglas, 73 (below): USAF, 74–75: Rockwell, 75: General Dynamics, 76: General Dynamics, 77: Ford Aerospace, 78: USAF, 79 (both pictures): Grumman, 80: Grumman, 81: USAF, 82: Ferranti, 83: British Aerospace, 84 (top): Rolls Royce, 84–85: Dassault Breguet, 85 (top): SAAB, 86: McDonnell Douglas, 87: US Navy, 88–89: Vought, 88 (below): McDonnell Douglas, 88 (top): General Dynamics, 89: General Dynamics, 90: US Navy, 91 (top): Lockheed, 91 (below): Sikorsky, 92–93: McDonnell Douglas, 94–95: Lockheed, 96: USAF, 97 (top): Lockheed, 97 (below): USAF, 98–99: Hughes Helicopters, 100: Westland, 101 (top): Bell, 101 (below left): MBB, 101 (below right): US Army, 102 (top): Boeing Vertol, 102 (below): Bell, 103: Hughes Helicopters, 104–105: Sikorsky, 105 (right): Bell, 105 (left): Boeing Vertol, 107: Martin Marietta, 108: USAF, 109: DoD, 110–111: Boeing, 112: Vought, 113: Hughes Aircraft, 114–115: USAF, 116: USAF, 117: Martin Marietta, 118: Israeli Aircraft Industries, 119: Canadair, 120–121: Lockheed, 123: Lockheed, 124–125: Airbus Industrie, 126–127: Boeing, 127: Airbus Industrie, 128: Fokker, 129: Flight, 130: British Aerospace via Flight, 131: United Technologies, 133: Airbus Industrie, 134–135: Lockheed, 136: Press Association, 137: Aeritalia, 138: NASA, 141: Lockheed, 143: Rutan, 144: Rutan, 145: Rutan, 148–149: OMAC (via Flight), 148–149: Flight, 150–151: Rutan, 152–153: Flight, 154: National Air and Space Museum.

Campbell Rawkins and The Research House would like to thank all those organisations and individuals in aerospace and systems manufacturers, in government departments, in the services and in the press who have supplied the illustrations for this book.